HOW TO
GET IT
Right

HOW TO
GET IT
Right

Being Single, Married, Divorced, and Everything in Between

Alexys V. Wolf

How to Get It Right

Scripture quotation marked "NAS" are taken from the New American Standard Bible, Copyright 1960, 1962, 1968, 1971, 1972, 1973, 1975, 1977, 1995 by The Lockman Foundation. Used by permission. All rights reserved.

The opinions expressed by the author are those of The Fiery Sword Global Ministries.

Cover design by Rebeccacovers of FIVERR
Interior design by Aalisha of FIVERR
Editor Pamela Scholtes

Library of Congress Control Number: 2014914362

The Fiery Sword Publications
Lexington, SC 29073

Published in the United States of America

ISBN-13: 978-1530435678 (Paperback)
ISBN-13: 979-8802468135 (Hardcover)
ISBN-10: 1530435676

1. Religion / Christian Life / Personal Growth
2. Religion / Christian Life / Spiritual Growth

Dedication

Michael

Table of Contents

Endorsements

Alexys Wolf's new book – *How to Get it Right: Being Single, Married, Divorced and Everything in Between* is thought-provoking, stimulating, packed with insight, and a pleasure to read. Prepare to be challenged. You need not concur with her every conclusion or interpretation to profit from the author's wisdom. Her views are grounded in a profound knowledge of Scripture and reverence for God's Word. The enemy of truth is often not change but tradition. Appropriately, Wolf approaches marriage and divorce with what might be called a biblically Christian as opposed to a traditionally religious view. Sadly, many today who call themselves *"Christians"* base their beliefs and model their behavior on the world's standards, not on Scripture. Alexys V. Wolf is forthright in confronting these failings, mincing no words in upholding Biblical standards of purity. Refreshingly honest and open in sharing her own heartbreaking experiences, with candor and humility she tells a compelling, human story of God's grace and redemption. ~ ***Author Walter Brian Cisco***

WOW! This book is full of wisdom and insight that I've never heard taught in any church. It will take you from the beginning where God ordained a specific man for a specific woman, all the way to Holy Matrimony. *How to Get it Right* gives you the knowledge to *"get it right"* the first time and clarifies the error of some current beliefs.

Even if you already missed the mark, here you will find revelation as to how to move forward in God's will. I thank God for Alexys and her honesty and Holy Spirit leading as she is a gift to all of us. **~ Pamela Scholtes, editor**

How to Get It Right is a book needed for such a time as this. So many friends and family are scarred and live broken, defeated lives due to divorce. So many hurt and don't understand why. It is also needed for us old married folks. It reminds us of our vows and commitment. It is refreshing to see an author that is not afraid to *"bare all"* to help others in their search for truth and healing. After many years, it was a real treat to reacquaint myself with Alexys and to read this manuscript. This book is for everyone because we all need the information and healing contained in these pages. Alexys explains soul ties, divorce, and true forgiveness as I have never read. It is my pleasure to recommend this book. **~ Carole F. Crosby**

How to Get it Right is one of the best books I have ever read on all the deep questions involved in this topic. It does more than just provide opinions; it gives Scripture to look at concerning these various issues. This isn't a fluffy book filled with data; instead, it is a hard-hitting, thought-provoking book that gives honest answers and things to consider for your own life. The section on covenant is awesome! There is a way to be healthy within a marriage and God must be first and foremost for that to occur. Author Alexys V. Wolf shares personal experiences that help the reader relate to and come alongside her in her quest for knowledge. **~ Cheryl Kelly**

Foreword

Once in a while, you meet someone who can only be described as someone of the utmost integrity and rock solid. If you ask them a question, the one person you know will not give you an opinionated response but an answer only found by studying and searching out the unadulterated Word of God. Alexys V. Wolf has 'studied and certainly showed herself approved as a workman that need not be ashamed.

When Alexys first asked me to write a foreword for another one of her books, first and foremost, I was very excited to be able to read yet another of her manuscripts to dive into her findings and explorations of the heart and Word of God. When she told me the original title of *"Marriage, Divorce, and Restoration,"* it was then I felt utterly unqualified. Throughout the whole manuscript, I never doubted I should be reading the book and learning from her knowledge and candid openness and honesty about her own life and *"nightmares"* and her depth of truth found in Scripture. You see, I've been going through my own outlandish point in time. My own divorce was just finalized in early 2012. I came across something Alexys said that literally summed up my very thoughts as I read on. As I determined in my fleshly man to be strong, I was still, and I quote, *"nothing more than weakness veiled."*

Don't wait to go through a divorce or after the fact to read this book, but pass it on to newlyweds. In fact, give it to your single friends. We have to understand His Word regarding all aspects of marriage, grasp the magnitude of the marriage covenant, and comprehend and value the vows we so eagerly speak with no understanding or regard thereof. It truly doesn't matter if we agree with divorce or marriage. Alexys, as always, explores and digs deeply into the Scriptures. You will be challenged in your opinions, beliefs, and theologies you've created with half-truths. People are destroyed for lack of knowledge—marriages are destroyed, and, more so, restoration is aborted from lack of knowledge of His Word and will.

If you're like I, you're already thinking of the Scripture where it declares *"God hates divorce,"* thinking it shouldn't take place, regardless. You can't hate something if you haven't experienced it. God has experienced it firsthand. Yes, He hates it the same as He hates to see many things. Therefore, He can also get you through it. You have not surprised Him. There is a reason why we have an Old Covenant and a New Covenant.

Many write about marriage based on opinion, unlived realities, and not looking into the intended meanings of Scriptures. However, few dare to seek the truth of the Word regardless of their own beliefs reliving their own nightmares laying it out so that others may live wholly in certainty and learn from His intended truths. If only our commitment would first be to the Lord and seeking His will for our lives instead of allowing ourselves to get caught up in the emotions of marriage or a relationship, our commitment would be first to Truth despite what it might mean for us. Imagine the lives and relationships we could then have.

Today is the day to put down our cultivated half-truths, religiosity, legalism, judgments, and closed-mindedness. Hear what the Spirit is honestly saying. You're reading this for a reason. Maybe it's just so you don't wrongfully pass judgment on the *"Christian family"* next door. Perhaps it's to see into yourself to avoid a catastrophic relationship altogether or to give you the strength and assurance to break free from your nightmare sans condemnation. This one thing I know for sure—His Word always gives life. It is a plumb line upon which we can measure every decision. However, the key is understanding and knowledge of His Word with accuracy. We need to give honor where honor is due and genuinely appreciate God's ambassadors, such as Alexys V. Wolf, who won't settle for misinformation or lack of understanding. Those that insist on knowing what His Word really states, setting people free and changing lives. Thank you, Alexys, for yet another powerful journey into God's Truth, His will, and His intent. ~ *Carrie S. King, Ontario, Canada*

Introduction

Mere commitment puts you in control; surrender to your spouse puts them in control. "Surrender to God" means God is in control instead of self-will. Before you baulk at such a statement, remember that surrender won't make you a doormat but a compliment to the one who equally surrenders to you in a holy marriage. Commitment to your marriage can come and go leaving divorce optional based on nothing more than *"I'm unhappy."* Surrendering one to another leaves no leeway for divorce, only resolution. We are to submit in marriage one to another. This statement should awaken us to understand the gravity of marital covenant. In this understanding, one will be much less likely to marry in the first place and will willingly wait upon their pre-ordained mate. This brings us back to total surrender to God to be spiritually prepared to surrender to the one for whom you were created before the Earth's foundation.

When I was young, I had no idea what to expect from marriage, the meaning of the marriage covenant, how to fall in love with God first, how to discern and hear God's voice, or that God created me specifically for one man just as He created Eve specifically for Adam. None of this was anywhere on my spiritual radar. All I knew was that one day I would marry and that I wanted a house and a few kids. Beyond that, I was totally oblivious! After two failed marriages between twenty and thirty years old, and now happily married to my ordained husband, I have a few nuggets of helpful information to share with those willing to read it. I have learned a few things about marriage and what God says about it, as well as His meaning.

In Matthew 23:4, Jesus states the religious and self-righteous, «*They tie up heavy burdens and lay them on men's shoulders, but they themselves are unwilling to move them with so much as a finger.*" Although we should not be astonished this is happening today, it is within modern-day churches. Leaders and laymen alike set many standards fraught with condemnation and guilt. So it is with divorce. It is a raw and misinterpreted area where many refuse to extend mercy and grace, yet all the while, they withhold their own iniquities [sin]. This book is for anyone single, married, or divorced, currently considering marriage or divorce, or anyone who is happily married or single but may one day consider marriage or divorce. In one sentence, it's for anyone who desires earnestly to be in the center of God's will regarding their present or future mate.

I pray for God's people to become enlightened concerning marriage and divorce so we can all be free where we are. There are far too many unholy marriages we attempt to save, and too many holy marriages we are too quick to dissolve. Without a shadow of a doubt, there are way too many single people preparing to one day enter marriage sans a clue what God has ordained marriage to be, what they must take into marriage, or what they should expect from marriage. I do not claim to know everything, but what I do know is worth exploring. May YHWH, our Great God, enlighten us all so we may better serve, honor, and glorify Him.

CHAPTER 1

God's Perspective

"When you brought in foreigners, uncircumcised in heart and uncircumcised in flesh, to be in My sanctuary to profane it, even My house, when you offered My food, the fat and the blood; for they made My covenant void—this in addition to all your abominations (Ezekiel 44:7)."

Understanding God's View:

God hates divorce; however, we need to clarify what type of divorce is hated. God understands divorce, for God has been divorced, as noted in Ezekiel 44:7. To *"make My covenant void"* is to divorce. He divorced His holy Bride in times past due to her harlotry and deep-seated wickedness. God wants His people to view both marriage and divorce, not from the perspective of Law, but from His heart. He is Law, but He sent His Son to fulfill the Law mankind was incapable of fulfilling; therefore, we must look at things as a whole instead of in fragments.

Eunuch for the Kingdom of God:

Marriage is a physical depiction of our spiritual union [marriage] with God. In Matthew 19:11-12, Jesus says, *"Not all men can accept this statement, but only those to whom it has been given. For there are eunuchs who were born that way from their mother's womb; and there are eunuchs who were made eunuchs by men; and there are also eunuchs who made themselves eunuchs for the sake of the Kingdom of Heaven. He who is able to accept this, let him accept it."*

A eunuch, by man's definition, is a *"castrated human male."* Spiritually speaking, since the Spirit is neither male nor female, either gender can be a eunuch in so much as they choose to abstain from sex for the greater good of God's Kingdom. It could be one who has homosexual tendencies, but they vow to God to abstain for the sake of the Kingdom of Heaven. It could be a sex addict who, for the sake of God's Kingdom, abstains altogether, and so on.

We should be so in love with God that obedience is our desire, not our burden. This comes from trust in who He is. In this, we want [desire, long] to submit because His ways are best. Unfortunately, even when we possess the earnest desire for obedience, we rarely know what true obedience is. We must all keep in mind that not all people are meant to marry, but whether we are or are not, there is always a plan. If the one called to be a eunuch can accept it, they should seek YHWH to give them peace, joy, and understanding of their God-ordained purpose.

Divorce Hope:

If, on the other hand, one is to marry, God specifically creates their mate so that, when the two come together, they perfectly unify with one another and God. In this, God is honored, and the people are richly blessed. There are countless marriages not of God but of man. To open this first chapter, I have inserted the following excerpt from *Divorce Hope* to lend insight from someone else's marriage and divorce point of view:

> We have heard this Scripture: "Yahweh God of Israel says that HE HATES DIVORCE" (Malachi 2:16). This is almost

always quoted as if God hates all divorces in general. But that's just not true. We have previously read from the Bible books of Ezra, Nehemiah, Jeremiah, Deuteronomy and 1 Corinthians that God is not against divorce. Then why all the confusion concerning why God said that "He hates divorce?" The reason for the confusion is because there are TWO "kinds" of marriages and TWO "divorces" being mentioned in the Malachi 2:11-16 passage.

The "divorces" were not official divorces; they didn't need to be. They were already previously married and "unofficially" married again. The Hebrew word shalach means "putting away"—a separation, as correctly translated in most Bibles. However, the King James and a number of newer versions have incorrectly translated shalach as to mean: divorce. It never meant divorce and it doesn't mean divorce. The word was most likely translated as "divorce" to fit what was taught in the church. Shalach is just a common word used throughout the Old Testament which means to: go, separate or to send. That's it!

So why did God angrily say that He "...hated putting away [a separation]?" "...Because you have not kept My ways [concerning marriage, divorce and remarriage] but have SHOWN PARTIALITY IN THE LAW" (Malachi 2:9). The Law specifically stated that when a man got a divorce from his wife that he was to write "...her a CERTIFICATE OF DIVORCE, put it in her hand, AND [shalach] send her out [put her away]..." (Deuteronomy 24:1). God also commanded them not to marry anyone who did not serve Him — who served a foreign god (See Nehemiah 13:25-30). Instead, men separated from their wives without ever giving them a Certificate of Divorce and then illegally married someone else. This is why Yahweh said that they were still "their wife by covenant." The marriage covenant had never been dissolved by the Divorce Certificate.

"Yahweh's holy institution which He loves...Yahweh has been witness between you and the wife of your youth... [and] SHE [STILL] IS YOUR COMPANION AND YOUR WIFE BY COVENANT. For Yahweh God of Israel says that He hates divorce [shalach], [separating without a Certificate of Divorce].... He has [illegally] married the daughter of a foreign god. May Yahweh cut off...the man who does this being awake and aware." Malachi 2:11,12a,14b,c,16a

Because these men had remarried illegally — separated from their wives without giving them a Certificate of Divorce, they were in adultery as Jesus stated: "Furthermore it has been said, "Whoever PUTS AWAY [separates from {apoluo}] his wife, LET HIM GIVE HER A CERTIFICATE OF DIVORCE. But I say to you that whoever PUTS AWAY [separates and remarries without being divorced from] his wife for any reason except sexual immorality causes her to commit adultery: and whoever marries a woman who is PUT AWAY [separated without being divorced {apoluo}] commits adultery" (Matthew 5:31-32). (Yahweh never forgot about the Malachi incident when He came to Earth to redeem lost man). The Old Testament Hebrew word shalach and the New Testament Greek word <u>apoluo</u> are equivalent which will be discussed later.

Because these disobedient men still had "un-divorced" wives, Yahweh did not command them to give their illegal wives a Certificate of Divorce, rather, they simply had to "separate, put them away, [shalach]." SO DID GOD HATE DIVORCE? NO! RATHER, GOD HATED THAT THE HUSBANDS WERE SEPARATING FROM THEIR WIVES WITHOUT GIVING THEM A CERTIFICATE

OF DIVORCE WHICH WOULD ENABLE THEM TO
GET REMARRIED. THIS IS WHAT GOD HATES!

The men of Israel were SEPARATING from their wives
for self-gratifying reasons. God Himself was a "witness" at
their original marriage ceremony which was still in effect.
The marriage covenant was never dissolved by a Certificate
of Divorce. The men remarried outside their own culture
and tribe. God considered the children they bore unholy because of the mixed marriages bringing curses into their fam-
ilies (See Ezra 9:1,2; Nehemiah 13:26-30).

Because of these unauthorized marriages, the Word of
God came to Ezra and Nehemiah to have the men and wom-
en of Israel who had done this thing, to separate from their
spouse and even from their children (See Ezra 9:1, 11-12,
10:3, Nehemiah 13:23-27). In this situation, God's command
was to "put them away, separate yourselves from them!" This
was NOT the kind of marriage to which God was saying, "I
hate divorce!" He was saying loudly, "Get out of these wrong
marriages!"

DIVORCE IS A METHOD TO SEPARATE THE
ONE, AND MAKE THEM INTO TWO just as a surgeon's
knife is used to separate the cancerous flesh from the healthy
flesh. Both operations are good. Divorce can be used to kill
a righteous marriage, just as a surgeon's knife can be used to
kill a healthy person. (end excerpt from *Divorce Hope*)

Narrowing the Margin of Error:

Whether you agree or disagree, we still must understand that divorce
happens to Christians and non-Christians alike. So, instead of passing
judgment, let's find out how to prevent divorce as well as recover from
one. It can easily be prevented by understanding before marriage
that God does not have one hundred people in front of you, saying,
"*All these people love Me. Pick one.*" God is strategic in all things. To

be "unequally yoked" does not mean you are forbidden to marry someone of another race, color, nationality, or denomination. Instead, it's about who God created specifically for you to become one—one God pre-ordained you to honor Yahweh through the union. This definitely narrows the margin of possibilities!

If God's people understood this fundamental truth, we would not allow ourselves to be deceived, led by the flesh, and drawn into fleshly marriages. With understanding, there would be a considerable decrease in divorces since there would be a decrease in marriages. There would be more marriages of "*what God* has brought together." People marry for many reasons other than seeking God's face: sex, physical attraction, money, power, loneliness, rebound, rebellion, loyalty, parent-pleasing, parent-rebelling, pregnancy, to cover homosexuality, covering fornication, etc.—and all within the body of Christ. Even if both people are Christ-followers, that doesn't mean the two should marry. When things go wrong, we make messes and question why God made such a mess. We need to seek God's face concerning our ordained spouse, and then wait on God's instruction.

Notes

CHAPTER 2

Questions and Answers

Coming Unglued:

Many years ago, I heard it said that when you permanently glue two pieces of wood together, even if you forcefully pry them apart, wood fragments pieces remain permanently bonded to the other. So it is with divorce. One is never wholly free from the other because there are memory fragments of memories forever remaining.

I am twice divorced, once from an abusive, vile, adulterous husband and once from a great guy. In my second marriage, the nice one, I was in my own turmoil from the abuse of the first marriage. I am now married to the man for whom God created me before the foundation of the Earth. Even after forgiveness—receiving God's for self and extending it to ex-spouses—and repentance of my wrong along the way, some fragments will forever remain. This is not God's punishment, but rather God's Law in effect. It's simply the result of being two people glued together with someone with permanent glue [covenant vows] and ripping ourselves apart [broken covenant].

Some divorces must happen. Without getting into a debate, this is about the pain of a fallen world and bad choices. In the grand scheme of things, its evident that few marriages are actually God-ordained. Regardless of ones personal take on this subject, divorce happens. Even when I counsel people and agree divorce is necessary, I caution them that divorce is never an easy out. Divorce is never easy. It is both frightening and emotionally draining. The individuals must determine which route will usher true healing between themselves and God. Sometimes, it's working it out through great sacrifice, dedication, and seeking God's face. Still, other times, it is divorce for the sake of coming back to sanity, safety, healing, and peace.

If single people—divorced or never married—would grasp the magnitude of the marriage covenant, they would not so readily jump in. Married people, likewise, would not so readily jump out. Even after the pain of wounds has healed, the scars are permanent no matter how far in time and space you move. No one can dictate who someone should or shouldn't marry or who should or should not divorce. That is between the individuals and God.

We must, however, caution people of the ramifications of both. Every situation is different. There are Scriptures we could all debate and toss around, but it still comes back to the individual and their walk with God. Let us not forget that we all desperately need the free gift of grace [good we do not deserve] and mercy [not getting deserved punishment].

Q and A:

I have a dear friend and brother-in-Christ who posed some excellent marriage thoughts and questions. They are as follows:

1. I have questions about your belief that there's but one God-ordained person that He wants each of us to find and marry. Rather than that being a comforting thought [that God created someone just for me], in the emotional cauldron of dating [courtship], I'd be terrified of picking the wrong person,

knowing that getting it wrong would doom me to a life of marital misery.

Of course, we should want God's perfect will for our lives and need to pray for direction in these most critical decisions. Christians are under orders to marry only other believers; that much we know. I remember my teen leader's warning, "*Don't date someone you already know you couldn't marry.*" Adhering to that would preclude a lot of unnecessary risks. And I hear what you're saying about people marrying someone with whom they are having an affair or cohabitating. What have they gained once they tie the knot? A spouse they already know is more than willing to have sex outside of marriage—what a catch!

2. But why would God tell Christians to marry only believers if the choice was not ours to make? Wouldn't it be more consistent if the Bible said, «*Determine who it is that God has created for you, then marry them.*" We consider so many other issues in choosing a life partner, variables such as compatibility—what we think is important, what we have in common, and practicality—kids, money, health, etc. Still, a Christian hoping to marry may find themselves with more than one suitable choice. Could it be that God would bless a marriage to any one of them, as long as we don't knowingly disobey Him? Can we assume that all marriages that break up failed because it wasn't a union with that one, God-ordained person? Or that happy, successful, God-honoring marriages are impossible if we mistakenly choose the one who was not God's top choice for us?

My response to "*fear of messing up*" is this that we must understand, when we draw so near unto God's face and heart, mess-ups are fewer and farther between. This knowledge should usher *peace*, not *anx-*

iety. Fear comes from punishment, but perfect love casts out fear (I John 4:18). The more in love with Yahweh we grow, the less room fear will have a place to live and mutate into a spiritual paraplegic.

More often than not, we are looking for a mate rather than looking for the perfect will of God to manifest through our lives. With that frame of mind, we're already off course. When we do find someone we desire to marry, we generally don't seek God to answer the qestion *"Are they right or wrong?"* We only ask God to bless the union, regardless of His will. If we spend our time focused on God's perfect will instead of *"Who can I marry,"* everything will change. Instead of seeking a mate, we should seek God's Kingdom and righteousness (Matthew 6:33).

Simply stated, when God's people seek Him first and His mission set before us, we'll stop focusing on, *"What if I mess up? What if I do the wrong thing or want to marry the wrong person."* We will begin focusing on the Kingdom—supernaturally-naturally—our ordained mate will be presented and, through Holy Spirit already in full force, we will know the difference in time. Satan will send decoys along the route to throw us off the spiritual scent. Still, keen discernment from Holy Spirit actively moving within us will allow discernment to kick in and overpower the emotions and lusts of the fleshly man. It's as simple as that. The biggest problem with God's people is that we have grown as impatient as the world in need of Christ. Whether we want to acknowledge it or not, the fact remains.

I will address the question, *"Could it be that God would bless a marriage to any one of them, as long as we don't knowingly disobey Him? Can we assume that all marriages that break up failed because it wasn't a union with that one God-ordained person or that happy, successful, God-honoring marriages are impossible if we mistakenly choose the one who was not God's top choice for us?"*

I do not believe that just because a marriage breaks it was not of God. We have the innate ability to ruin the best of things, marriages included. Also, I don't believe that God can never bless a union that was not His perfect will. That would imply that something is impossible for God. Everything God has done on behalf of mankind works around our foolish mistakes. If the two people earnestly desire to be pleasing in His sight, God can manifest any number of miracles.

Also, I would like to add that certain people are for certain seasons, whether it pertains to marriage or other relationships. A person may very well have two ordained mates, but obviously separately in different seasons. Say someone marries a person ordained for them, but die prematurely. That does not mean that since they were their created mate, there won't be another season, post-healing, for their second ordained mate to come along. However, there is a possibility they are to remain celibate as a eunuch for the rest of their life. These are very intimate issues that need to be resolved between the individual and God. Again, when the focus remains on the Kingdom of Heaven in every season, there isn't much room for error.

3. His next question, "*What are the acceptable reasons for getting married? How does your 'one ordained mate' theory square with Paul's warning that those who 'burn with passion'—to Christ-followers—should go on and get married* (1 Corinthians 7:9)?" In I Corinthians 7:26-28, Paul says that when it comes to marrying or staying single, we're to count the cost, choose wisely, honor whatever commitments we've already made, then go ahead and decide based on those considerations. He doesn't seem to have a one-reason, one-person view. If so, wouldn't it be more logical to say, "*Pray for God to show you if He wants you to marry. If the answer is yes, ask Him to point out the one*"?

Good question, indeed, and not without an answer. I respond by skipping to verses 32-35, which read, "*But I want you to be free from concern. An unmarried one is concerned about the things of Yahweh, how he may please Yahweh; but one who is married is concerned about the things of the world, how he may please his wife, and his interests are divided. The unmarried woman, and the virgin, is concerned about the things of Yahweh, that she may be holy both in body and spirit; but one who is married is concerned about the things of the world, how she may please her husband. This I say for your own benefit; not to put a restraint upon you, but to promote what is appropriate and to secure undistracted devotion to Yahweh."*

With this in mind, for me, it only solidifies the relevance of God-ordained spouses. Paul speaks candidly that if you cannot control yourself in your *«burning*," marry, but with the marriage, your interests will be divided between Yahweh and your spouse. However—this is a large *"however*," if we conduct ourselves in self-discipline, as we are repeatedly instructed in I Corinthians 9:27, and wait upon the perfect will of Yahweh for our mate, how beautiful a union! In this, both the husband and the wife are focused on God together; hence, no division. Both will be so Kingdom-focused, Kingdom-minded, and Kingdom-driven that everything else will fall into its proper place. In this, they have secured undistracted devotion to the Lord while married.

Sadly, as it stands today, we burn. Therefore, in the effort to not commit fornication—the wrong motive for marriage, we enter a covenant not ordained by God; He merely allows it. Let's face facts, we live in a world where followers of Christ and non-followers conduct themselves in the same manner, leaving us all bewildered and hazy on God's will. People in and out of the body of Christ are committing adultery and fornication as though it is absolutely acceptable.

Many reason within themselves, *"God will forgive me."* But, as I've stated in previous books, forgiveness is not the issue. Forgiveness was given at the death, burial, and resurrection of Jesus. God's blessings, on the other hand, are the issue. When we do whatever we want and then expect God to bless any ol' marriage based on Apostle Paul's words, we limit His hand of blessings. We forge a mess without even realizing what we've done until the mess has fully metastasized.

Once we finally get on board with God's perfect will [obedience] versus His permissive will [disobedience], we are left in a bit of a quandary, the preverbal pickle, wondering why God forsook us. It does not have to be this way. Granted, God can absolutely bless wrong marriages if both the husband and wife choose submission to God and one another, but it must be a joint, unified decision that happens next to never. Most simply continue co-existing until death and call it a "*successful marriage*," all the while condemning those who "*didn't go the distance.*" "God loves the individuals who make up the marriage more than He loves the marriage institution!" states author Stephen Gola in his book *Divorce: God's Will?*

> "And we know that God causes all things to work together for good to those who *love* God, to those who are called according to His purpose (Romans 8:28)."

Prayer:

Father, as I read this book, I pray to understand what You want me to personally apply to my life. I desire to know what You know and understand what You understand. I thank You for helping me move out of the normal thinking of man's traditions and step into a new dimension of revelation that I may walk in freedom and holiness as You have designed for Your people. Amen.

Notes

CHAPTER 3

Understanding Covenant

"That they may all be one; even as You, Father, are in Me and I in You, that they also may be in Us, so that the world may believe that You sent Me (John 17:21)."

If God's holy people do not understand the covenant we have in the spirit realm between God and His people, we don't stand a chance of understanding the covenant between a man and a woman in marriage. This chapter is taken from my first book, *What Was God Thinking? Why Adam Had To Die,* chapter 7, *"Enter the Blood Covenant."*

I believe it to be of the utmost importance to help us understand what God has done for mankind. Once we obtain a reasonable concept of the spiritual-marital covenant, we will better grasp physical-marital covenant. Christ calls us to *"die daily"* spiritually so that our flesh does not impede our relationship with the Father, Son, and Holy Spirit—The Groom. In like fashion, we must *"die daily"* to our selfish nature to become *"one"* with our spouse to not hinder our relationship with our spouse—our physical bride or groom. If you've already read, *What was God Thinking?,* this chapter will simply be a refresher course.

Covenant Protection:

> "For where a covenant is, there must of necessity be the death of the one who made it. For a covenant is valid only when men are dead, for it is never in force while the one who made it lives (Hebrews 9:16-17)."

I consigned myself back to Christ in February of 2000, after seven years of angry rebellion. However, too quickly, I found myself right back in my fleshly ways resembling that of my rebellion. The result was becoming pregnant by a man that was not my husband. Our relationship was brief because I was quickly convicted, though not quickly enough, of my sinful conduct. However, my covenant covering [Holy Spirit] was removed by broken covenant.

Although God's love for me never moved, the removal of His covenant protection was a result of my blatant disobedience. I was no longer living according to the Spirit but dead flesh. I reactivated my soul instantly through lustful thinking, allowing it to override the voice of Holy Spirit speaking into my spirit. I liken the fleshly nature to a zombie in sci-fi movies. Though the person they once were is dead, as a zombie, the body moves at will, all the while destroying everything in its wake.

It is of the utmost urgency to know, accept, and understand that one cannot enter into the blood covenant Christ freely offers until we choose death to the fleshly nature. Death activates God's covenant. Disobedience [an act of the flesh] nullifies it. Man's flesh cannot enter into a covenant because of its cursed condition. Nothing impure can come into covenant with the pure and holy God. This is why Christ baptized the flesh of all mankind into the grave with Him. He crucified mankind to allow us free access to the Kingdom of God. As we take up our cross, we accept death as the only entrance into the holy covenant. Although we're technically already dead, our acknowledgment is required. Because Jesus is the last sacrifice and He shed His blood, we cannot receive His blood until we are purged of Adam's old blood.

Spiritually speaking, we must relinquish our old, condemned blood to receive the new pureblood. Christ's blood was shed so that we may receive it. We are not obligated, and we all have the right to keep our own. But, in doing so, we keep death eternal. God says in Deuteronomy that we choose life or death, blessings or curses. If we choose to keep our blood, we choose a curse. We choose life only when we choose His life-giving blood, His covenant of blessing.

It is of the utmost importance to understand dying to the flesh to validate and activate covenant with God. Merely saying the sinner's prayer may grant access to Heaven upon death of the physical body, but if the individual does not accept that they must die to their natural man and the desires thereof, that person will never truly enter into covenant with Yahweh. To reiterate, Christ crucified the flesh of all of mankind rendering it dead. When we live according to the flesh [death], we give false life to a dead thing causing much destruction.

As a side note, in the Old Testament, when God entered covenant with Noah, Abraham, Isaac, Phinehas, and David, no one died, at least not immediately. Every covenant about which we read in the Old Testament was made with a view to the Cross. God sees the end from the beginning, and the Word clearly states that Christ was slain from the foundation of the Earth (Revelation 18:3). All covenants foreshadowed the eternal covenant yet to come because what was "*yet to come*" was, in God's view, already completed.

Forfeiture of Covenant Protection:

> Are we to continue in sin so that grace may increase…How shall we who died to sin still live in it? Or do you not know that all of us who have been baptized into Christ Jesus have been baptized into His death? Therefore we have been buried with Him through baptism into death, so that as Christ was

raised from the dead through the glory of the Father, so we too might walk in newness of life… knowing this, that our old self was crucified with Him, in order that our body of sin might be done away with, so that we would no longer be slaves to sin; for he who has died is freed from sin. Now if we have died with Christ…death no longer is master over Him…consider yourselves to be dead to sin, but alive to God in Christ Jesus (Romans 6:1-11).

When Christ-followers walk according to their old fleshly man, they forfeit their covenant protection. Until we realize that we must die daily rendering the flesh inactive, covenant promises and protection will elude us. When a person of Christ sins, they reason, *"God will forgive me."* Truth be told, they are already forgiven. Forgiveness was sealed at the cross—it is a non-issue. Breaking covenant with God, however, is an issue.

Are you wondering what's going wrong in your life in Christ despite religious conduct and good deeds? Maybe *"life"* isn't the problem—*death* is. Possibly, we haven't died to ourselves, and, more than likely, we didn't realize death was a requirement for covenant activation. I didn't know this for way too long.

We are called to die with Christ in His death. The *"newness of life"* comes only after we crucify our flesh. It occurs to me that when someone accepts the Savior's blood repenting of the sin nature, they automatically enter covenant with Yahweh. Unfortunately, many are saved for a long time before they understand that the covenant has not been activated because they have not died to their old nature or understand they need to. Some never understand. They continue having all the same problems before salvation because they have no idea who they are in Christ. It is like having a vault full of billions of dollars, yet it is untapped because they do not know it exists or don't know they have the key in their possession. So it is with the average believer—they forfeit for lack of knowledge and perish.

Most people never know their covenant promises with zero understanding how to tap into the limitlessness of God's power and authority to overcome obstacles. They never receive revelation about how to die with Him. Operating within the covenant always eludes them. I was this way until it was revealed to me. By "*revealed*," I simply mean I attained supernatural revelation. Too many Christians are flooded with knowledge sans revelatory understanding of the deepest meaning. I say again that there is no covenant activation without death of the fleshly nature. It is the death for which He calls us that ushers freedom from sin.

Understanding We've Already Died:

> "For the law of the Spirit of life in Christ Jesus has set you free from the law of sin and of death. For what the Law could not do, weak as it was through the flesh, God did: sending His Son in the likeness of sinful flesh and as an offering for sin, He condemned sin in the flesh (Romans 8:2-3)."

Judgment was the result of the sin of one man (Romans 5:15-19). This judgment came to all men. Judgment is upon all flesh whether we are good people or bad in the eyes of the world or self. It took only one sin to defile all. But, praise God, since it only took one man to bring condemnation, it took only one act of righteousness through One Man for all to be justified. One act of disobedience equals condemnation for all. One act of pure obedience equals justification [made righteous in God's sight] to all who receive.

Although we have no choice in being born into condemnation, we must choose to receive justification. In other words, our biological mothers could not choose for us at natural birth to be born into righteousness. It is a conscious act that must come from the individual. We must seek it. It is always available, but still, we must accept and receive it through free will. Since we were naturally born into condemnation, we now must be born [a separate birth] into supernatural justification and sanctification [action or process of making one holy].

Through His death and resurrection, Jesus Christ brought into the earthly realm the Blood Covenant. It is a better covenant than Abraham's. The remarkable thing is that we get the better covenant plus all the promises given to Abraham and his descendants. God has provided more than we can think or imagine. As an aside, I love what this Scripture reads: *"God did."* What the Law could not accomplish, what man could not accomplish, *God did!* He did not leave us without hope in our condemned state. He willingly fulfilled what could not be fulfilled through ordinary man.

The Blessed Covenant:

"'THIS IS THE COVENANT THAT I WILL MAKE WITH THEM AFTER THOSE DAYS, SAYS THE LORD: I WILL PUT MY LAWS UPON THEIR HEART, AND ON THEIR MIND I WILL WRITE THEM,' HE THEN SAYS, 'AND THEIR SINS AND THEIR LAWLESS DEEDS I WILL REMEMBER NO MORE.' NOW WHERE THERE IS FORGIVENESS OF THESE THINGS, THERE IS NO LONGER ANY OFFERING FOR SIN (Hebrews 10:16-18)."

"For this reason He is the mediator of a new covenant, so that, since a death has taken place for the redemption of the transgressions that were committed under the first covenant, those who have been called may receive the promise of the eternal inheritance (Hebrews 9:15)."

"It is not the children of the *flesh* who are children of God, but the children of the *promise* who are regarded as descendants (Romans 9:8)."

"Since a death has taken place," stated in Hebrews 9, we are to take up the cross [death] *with* Christ—the One who made the covenant already gave His life. If we are a member of the Body of Christ and

do not submit the flesh regularly, know that we are running around aimlessly to no avail. We are going through meaningless motions because they are of the flesh. Anything we do not from Holy Spirit instruction is wood, hay, and stubble to God—worthless from an eternal Kingdom, standpoint. We must care for our physical body because it is the temple of the Living God. However, we must be emptied of the sinful nature so that Holy Spirit may freely move through us and also that we may be free *with* Him and *in* Him. It is for our benefit as well as for the Kingdom of God.

The Scribes and Pharisees claimed to be "*descendants*" because they were in the physical bloodline of Abraham. This Scripture and others state that the Son's covenant comes through faith in Christ. The flesh has no covenant with God. It is our spirit that receives Christ through faith. All who enter into covenant with the Father are true descendants of Abraham and have access to all the promises given to and through him.

The Seal of Promise:

> "In Him, you also, after listening to the message of truth, the gospel of your salvation—having also believed, you were sealed in Him with the Holy Spirit of promise (Ephesians 1:13)."

> "Remember that you were at that time separate from Christ, excluded from the commonwealth of Israel, and strangers to the covenants of promise, having no hope and without God in the world (Ephesians 2:12)."

> "To be specific, that the Gentiles are fellow heirs and fellow members of the body, and fellow partakers of the promise in Christ Jesus through the gospel (Ephesians 3:6)."

Holy Spirit is the *"Seal of Promise,"* the mark of God. How will we be known by God lest we crucify our flesh? How will the demons know us? How will man know us? Two lives cannot rule in one body. The flesh of man is perpetually at war with the Spirit of God. Death to the worldly way of thinking and doing, the lusts of the flesh, brings us into covenant relationship with the Father, our Husband. It brings us access to all the covenant blessings but disobedience breaks covenant protection. This is why He calls us to die daily. He wants us to inherit all that is His, and He has instructed us how to attain it. He withholds nothing from us—it is we who withhold His hand.

Prayer:

I release myself to You totally and completely without reservation. Show me how to die daily to the fleshly nature in which I was originally born and how to allow Your Holy Spirit full access to all of me. Make me mindful that I am an heir to the Promise through Your Spirit and not through external actions of my flesh. I thank You, Jesus, that by Your stripes, I am healed, and by Your wounds, I have been transferred from death unto light. I bless You, Almighty, that You did not leave me abandoned but adopted me as a rightful heir to the Kingdom of God. Amen.

Notes

CHAPTER 4

The Covenant of Intercourse

Or do you not know that the unrighteous will not inherit the Kingdom of God? Do not be deceived; neither fornicators, nor idolaters, nor adulterers, nor effeminate, nor homosexuals…food is meant for the stomach and the stomach for food—and God will destroy both one and the other. The body is not meant for sexual immorality, but for Yahweh, and Yahweh for the body…Do you not know that your bodies are members of Christ? Shall I then take away the members of Christ and make them members of a prostitute? May it never be! Or do you not know that the one who joins himself to a prostitute is one body with her? For He says, "THE TWO SHALL BECOME ONE FLESH." But the one who joins himself to Yahweh is one spirit with Him. Flee immorality. Every other sin that a man commits is outside the body, but the immoral man sins against his own body. Or do you not know that your body is a temple of the Holy Spirit who is in you, whom you have from God, and that you are not your own? For you have been bought with a price: therefore glorify God in your body (1 Corinthians 6:9, 13, 15-20).

"Marriage is to be held in honor among all, and the marriage bed is to be undefiled; for fornicators and adulterers God will judge (Hebrews 13:4)."

We Make Our Messes:

When God's people choose to sexually give themselves to another outside the marriage covenant, they are essentially setting their bodies above God, making it and its desires an idol above God. Sex outside of marriage is a serious matter diminished to something seemingly harmless and sinless.

God has given us direction informing us about action consequences. When we sin against God, especially in this arena, first we revel in it; then, when the bad seed turns into a harvest, we wonder why God has forsaken us because it's too heavy to bear. We reason, "*I am a good person. Why did God let this happen?*" We must stop worshipping man—self or others—and placing anything or anyone above YHWH. Idolatry will always lead to a shattered life.

Understanding Intercourse:

Marriage is "*intimacy.*" Intimacy is "*communion;*" drawing as near to someone as possible, otherwise known as "*intercourse.*" Because this word, intercourse, is grossly underestimated, I have listed definitions:

Merriam-Webster Definition of Intercourse: 1. connection or dealings between persons or groups; 2. exchange especially of thoughts or feelings: communion; 3. sexual intercourse

Lexic.us Definition of Intercourse: 1. *Noun.* Communication between individuals; a commingling (to blend thoroughly into a harmonious whole); intimate connection or dealings between persons or nations, as in common affairs and civilities, in correspondence or trade; communication; commerce; especially, interchange of thought and feeling; association; communion; **2.** *Noun.* The act of sexual procreation between a man and a woman

Sex is merely one expression of intercourse; it is not intercourse itself. Sex was created by God to be a beautiful expression of covenant commitment that changed lives for the better. It is one form of life-changing covenant. Hence, sexual activity outside of marital covenant falls flat and leaves one empty and frustrated. There is a more significant void to someone after engaging in sex because there is no covenant unity. The people are left having become *"one body,"* yet devoid of covenant.

As it is now, sex is destroying lives because it has not been kept sacred. The world is now flooded with fatherless children, motherless children, and childless parents via abortion, abandonment, or adoption. Some teens are parents. Adult men and women are murdering their unborn and born children because they were conceived from fornication or adultery. Sexually transmitted diseases are running rampant because society has made sexual intercourse something for everyone and anyone. God did not create sex for this purpose, and we are all suffering at the hand of our selfish indulgence, negligence, lack of self-control, and abuse. God is not the problem—we are.

Marriage Covenant Requires Death:

As a chapter two recap, *"For where a covenant is, there must of necessity be the death of the one who made it. For a covenant is valid only when men are dead, for it is never in force while the one who made it lives,"* states Hebrews 9:16-17. Entering into marriage brings death to both individuals and recreates them as one new being. This is a requirement for true success, both in our spiritual marriage to God and physical marriage to people, yet it rarely happens due to our gross lack of covenant understanding. Refusing to die to self to activate covenant is disastrous for all involved! If dying to self seems extreme, understand that we don't fully enter into the marriage covenant until we do. In fact, when two people refuse to become selfless, their marriage covenant hasn't truly been activated.

Take a close look at the opening Scripture of this chapter. The act of sex makes two become one. To repeat, sexual activity was created as a bonding tool exclusively for marriage. It is one way, but not solely, for people to express unity, oneness—intercourse. It is designed to be a physical depiction of what happens spiritually with God. When we give ourselves to another human being in this capacity, we are uniting with them, be they our created mate or a random person we'll never see again. This is a serious act that, especially in this day and age, most people take lightly, including many within Christ's body.

Look at what happens when we have sexual intercourse outside of the bonds of holy matrimony. People become erratic, possessive, ashamed, needy, condemned, and they feel entitled to liberties with the other person even if they barely know one another. There is a *"clinginess"* that takes effect, especially for the woman. This is because she and he became *"one flesh,"* whether they understand it or not, like it or not. Sex is a spiritual form of superglue.

Generally speaking, the man becomes closed off and runs the other way. If there was a friendship, it flies out the window. Everything becomes awkward and uncomfortable. This is because they both gave and took what wasn't theirs to offer or receive. This is God's law in motion— *"two become one flesh."* It's like the law of sowing and reaping; reaping a bad harvest due to sin is not punishment but law in motion. So it is with sex outside of marriage.

The Rich Man's Riches:

> And someone came to Him and said, "Teacher, what good thing shall I do that I may obtain eternal life?" And He said to him, "Why are you asking Me about what is good? There is

only One who is good; but if you wish to enter into life, keep the commandments." Then he said to Him, "Which ones?" And Jesus said, "YOU SHALL NOT COMMIT MURDER; YOU SHALL NOT COMMIT ADULTERY; YOU SHALL NOT STEAL; YOU SHALL NOT BEAR FALSE WITNESS; HONOR YOUR FATHER AND MOTHER; AND YOU SHALL LOVE YOUR NEIGHBOR AS YOURSELF." The young man said to Him, "All these things I have kept; what am I still lacking?" Jesus said to him, "If you wish to be complete, go and sell your possessions and give to the poor, and you will have treasure in Heaven; and come, follow Me." But when the young man heard this statement, he went away grieving; for he was one who owned much property (Matthew 19:16-22).

In today's God-less society, I liken this rich man's riches to sex outside marriage. So many unmarried people want to go to church and be a *"good person,"* yet they refuse to give up sex that God ordained only for the marriage bed. Interestingly enough, the rich man asked which commands he was to follow. This infers he was interested in obliging only the minimum commands. He was not interested in giving all of himself to inherit the fullness of the Kingdom of God.

When I conduct pre-marital counseling, the first thing I ask is, *"Are you having sex outside of marriage?"* People hate this question! They hate it because they are guilty yet still ask God to bless their upcoming union. That's like asking your fiancé' to be faithful to you, yet every now and then, they must allow you to have an affair. We do not rightly seek God's favor when we refuse to obey His simple commands—it is a contradiction in every way.

Becoming One—Pros and Cons:

As previously mentioned, sex was designed marvelously by God to be an offshoot of a covenant seal, the glue that bonds two people together in holy matrimony. In the spirit realm, Holy Spirit inserted within our person is a form of intercourse. In other words, when we confess and repent of the sin nature, the water that ran from Jesus' side pours through us and washes us. Holy Spirit is inserted within, and then we are covered by Jesus' blood. Holy Spirit is our Seal of Promise of what is to come. We are "*in*" Him, and He is "*in*" us—intercourse. Through such intercourse, we bear His fruit and multiply Spirit's fruit. Such spiritual intercourse causes new births— offspring of the new union bonded through intercourse. Likewise, through sexual intercourse intimacy, mankind multiplies physically.

We can now understand that the problem comes when we become one with someone other than our spouse. Being married to someone God ordained for us before the foundation of the Earth bears *good* fruit. Children of such a union, generally speaking, are well-rounded and secure because they were produced through *holy* covenant. In this perverse generation, however, everyone is having sex with whomever, wherever, and whenever the mood strikes. This sin act bears fruit from that which is unholy, absent of covenant. As a result, there are whole generations confused, distressed, oppressed, bewildered, angry, depressed, lost, and so on because of their parents' lack of covenant. The Law of increase (Genesis 9:7) remains, but it produces negative seed instead of positive seed, and all of it multiplies.

Before we go any further, please know that I am *not* condemning people born out of wrong covenant or non-covenant. I am simply pointing out that most of these particular people are this way due to the manifestation of Gods Law in effect. God set the *Law of increase* [go forth and multiply]. Multiplication happens for the good when people are obedient to Gods commands. On the flip side, it negatively occurs when people disobey Gods commands.

Noting Hebrews 9:16-17 stating that covenant does not go into effect until men are dead, I conveyed that through marriage vows, two people must die to self and become one. There is no covenant when people engage in premarital sex because no one has died to activate the covenant. When this happens, and we procreate regardless, anger ensues because people have life responsibilities that should only come through covenant because covenant brings protection. Lack of covenant amid covenant responsibilities brings anguish.

Once all is said and done, we «*good Christians*» get angry at God because He didn't better protect us. We need to understand also that God cannot protect those who step outside His covenant boundaries. When we disobey God's commands, it stems from bringing our dead flesh back to a simulation of life. When we break covenant with Yeshua, we remove ourselves from His umbrella of protection.

It's simple, really. When man crucifies self and joins Christ, covenant is in effect—protection is activated. When we resurrect our fleshly cursed nature from Adam, though saved from hell, we break covenant with God and become unprotected. More specifically, when we engage in sex outside of the covenant bonds of marriage, we willfully enter territory unprotected with people who have no desire to protect us; or if they desire to protect, protection eludes them.

Notes

CHAPTER 5

Common Law "Marriage"

And those who are in the flesh cannot please God. However, you are not in the flesh but in the Spirit, if indeed the Spirit of God dwells in you. But if anyone does not have the Spirit of Christ, he does not belong to Him. If Christ is in you, though the body is dead because of sin, yet the spirit is alive because of righteousness. But if the Spirit of Him who raised Jesus from the dead dwells in you, He who raised Christ Jesus from the dead will also give life to your mortal bodies through His Spirit who dwells in you. So then, brethren, we are under obligation, not to the flesh, to live according to the flesh—for if you are living according to the flesh, you must die; but if by the Spirit you are putting to death the deeds of the body, you will live (Romans 8:8-13).

Two Become One:

For anyone who reasons, *"If I become one with someone through sexual intercourse and we are considered as married, what's the purpose of marriage? I don't need a certificate to validate my relationship. In the sight of God, we're already married,"* I direct them to Jesus' response to the Samaritan woman. In John 4:17-19, we read, *"The woman answered and said, 'I have*

no husband.' Jesus said to her, 'You have correctly said, "I have no husband,"
for you have had five husbands, and the one whom you now have is not your
husband; this you have said truly.' The woman said to Him, 'Sir, I perceive that
You are a prophet.'"

A couple items required addressing. Jesus said she correctly stated, "*I have no husband,*" yet she had five husbands before her current common-law husband. If she is five times divorced and Jesus made it known she didn't have a husband, she is cleared of still being married post-divorce. Secondly, though she was entering sexual relations with someone not her husband, Jesus did not consider that as marital validation in God's sight. God honored her granted divorces as no longer married, and equally, her common-law husband wasn't a husband at all.

Repeatedly, we see that marriage is the place of covenant—the only place God can and will honor sexual relations between a man and a woman. Sexual intercourse is to be kept holy as God intended. It is not for us to use as a tool to alleviate tension, validate a romantic relationship, or abuse in any capacity. Sex outside of marriage is a sin and extremely dangerous, much like a toddler with a butcher knife or loaded gun.

Biblical Dating?

The next question among followers of The Way [Christ] is, "*What is appropriate conduct in dating?*" Let's look at the next Bible passages:

> Now concerning the things of which you wrote to me: It is good for a man not to touch a woman. Nevertheless, because of sexual immorality, let each man have his own wife, and let each woman have her own husband. Let the husband render to his wife the affection due her, and likewise also the wife to her husband. The wife does not have authority over her own body, but the husband does. And likewise the husband does not have authority over his own body, but the wife does.

Do not deprive one another except with consent for a time, that you may give yourselves to fasting and prayer; and come together again so that Satan does not tempt you because of your lack of self-control (1 Corinthians 7:1-5, NKJV).

The phrase *"to touch a woman"* is an idiom referring to *"sexual relations."* *"Apto"* is the Greek word Paul uses for *"to touch."* It has the sense of touch, cling, take hold of; to kindle as in *"to kindle a fire."* It can mean any form of physical touch, from light caress to actual sexual intercourse.

Paul continues with the word *«nevertheless,"* which connects all he is saying. Dating is a western practice not found anywhere in the Bible. This would lead me to believe that dating as we know it in modern western society is invalid. With Paul's apt *"nevertheless,"* he instructs men and women to marry and then, as in post-marriage vows, conduct yourselves in any form of touch that is holy in God's sight.

Many argue that numerous issues are not mentioned in the Bible, but they do not constitute as sin, e.g. celebrating birthdays, Christmas, dating, etc. Some Scriptures specifically speak to relations between a man and woman negating modern-day dating. If *"dating"* simply meant spending quality time getting to know one another, that would be acceptable, but the excessive touching between unmarried couples is indeed sin.

Paul continues to instruct the married couple to not abstain from sex. Within marriage, the man and woman are no longer their own. They belong to each other. We can conclude from this one section of verses that touching within the confines of dating is not permitted. We all know that few, if anyone, will uphold God's way of thinking, sad as the fact is. If you must date, keep all body parts to yourself since the more two people touch, the more they *"burn."* They are tempted to forget God and act in the flesh—literally and metaphorically, which may lead to a marriage or some form of improper conduct that God never designed or ordained.

Cohabitation Debacles:

Living together, having sex before marriage, merging households without marriage—these are common occurrences in the modern-day Babylon in which we live. We've set such low precedence that no one, including Christians, seems to know right from wrong in any given situation, especially in the arena of romantic relationships.

During this books original writing, I attempted to help two men out of their unholy unwed unions. Both men felt trapped and struggled to see an exit. They were all miserable because none of the four entered their relationships in right standing with God. Yeshua was not consulted in the least. Because they were living in sin with their girlfriends, these men wedged themselves into the role of father to their girlfriends' children and husband to women not their wives. These four have played marriage while having no marital covenant—a recipe for disaster!

One fellow and his live-in girlfriend were both married to estranged spouses. He refused to get out of the relationship when it was suggested. Because he hesitated to do what was holy and helpful for everyone, he eventually became aggressive as they both would badger one another mentally, emotionally, and physically. As a result, now he's in jail. If only he'd been obedient to God to remove himself from an adulterous relationship, he'd not be in jail. He tried so hard to force something to work that couldn't, and it ended in a worse way than necessary. This guy was too worried about her kids because he was their only support that he missed Gods plan altogether.

Because of his emotional and financial ties to her children, he felt he couldn't leave, so he remained in an unhealthy, unholy, unhappy relationship ending worse than if he had just said, *"This isn't working. It isn't right in God's sight. We need to separate."* Fear became a factor; afraid of hurting her, hurting her kids, leaving them abandoned, etc. When fear is in play, wisdom cannot prevail. God's voice cannot be clearly heard or abided when fear is in action. Because of placing himself in a situation against God, fear became the lead causing nothing less than chaos and confusion.

The other gentleman has two children, and his girlfriend has a child; together, they've merged households for many years. He is acting as a father to her child, and she is serving as a mother to his children. Now he's trying to get his life aligned with Yeshua and feels stuck just like the other guy. He doesn't hate her, but he doesn't love her. They can't divorce because they're not legally married and he feels trapped in his own home. He positioned himself to become something [husband, father] he never was. They are "*common law*" married living illegally from fornication and lack of covenant in God's sight. He, too, is fearful of what will happen when and if he breaks the relationship as she and her child have nowhere to go.

My suggestion to them would be to align themselves with God and, in so doing, pull the plug on the very unhealthy relationship, stop having sex, stop living together and recalibrate from there. Fear is a terrible thing but always comes into action when lives are not aligned with the God who has already overcome fear. Imagine if they both began walking in surrender to Christ. They would no longer worry about the outcome, but only that they are living a holy lifestyle by God's commands. By recalibrating their thinking from an earthly, fleshly perspective into a heavenly, godly one, all fears would calm, and they would have faith to do what is correct, trusting that Yahweh will work things for good for all involved (Romans 8:28).

Those who live in common-law relationships miserable and sometimes volatile are setting a shallow bar of life for their kids. They worry that the kids will be hurt if they split, but I say they'll be hurt worse in the long run if they don't make an immediate change. Doesn't everyone want their children to grow in a home where the parent or parents are at peace, joyful, and walking per Christ's will? Living together unmarried will always, in time, lead to misery. The only exception is when the couple repents, aligns with Christ, and moves forward.

Happiness or Holiness:

> Therefore be imitators of God, as beloved children; and walk in love, just as Christ also loved you and gave Himself up for us, an offering and a sacrifice to God as a fragrant aroma. But immorality or any impurity or greed must not even be named among you, as is proper among saints; and there must be no filthiness and silly talk, or coarse jesting, which are not fitting, but rather giving of thanks. For this you know with certainty, that no immoral or impure person or covetous man, who is an idolater, has an inheritance in the kingdom of Christ and God. Let no one deceive you with empty words, for because of these things the wrath of God comes upon the sons of disobedience (Ephesians 5:1-6).

> For this is God's will, your sanctification; that is, that you abstain from sexual immorality; that each of you know how to possess his own vessel in sanctification and honor, not in lustful passion, like the Gentiles who do not know God (I Thessalonians 4:3-5).

> "Now those who belong to Christ Jesus have crucified the flesh with its passions and desires (Galatians 5:24)."

Neither immorality nor impurity should be named among God's people. These texts are life-altering. Far too many people are concerned more with personal happiness than holiness before God, and it should not be. Guilt is involved when feeling selfish and seeking such happiness. In this state of guilt, the concept of holiness is swept under the rug.

Imagine a person completely surrendered to God. This person will no longer seek happiness, nor will they be led by emotions of guilt, shame, fear, or anything else. On the other hand, they will be focused solely on pleasing the Savior. There is no room for anything other than holiness; they'll do whatever it takes to be in direct obedience to the One who can resolve any matter. A person, such as the two men mentioned above, would be able to make clear, concise decisions concerning their own personal lives. They would be able with ease to tell their girlfriends that, since they're seeking the face and holiness of Christ, they must, of necessity, break the union, or at the very least, stop living in sin. Their desire for holiness would cause them to surrender completely to Christ and, in so doing, do whatever necessary to follow Christ.

One must understand that *"commitment"* and *"surrender"* are vastly different. *"Commitment"* in or to anything means you are the one in control; you can quit whenever you want. *"Surrender,"* adversely, denotes one not in control. You can't stop because you no longer have a say or vote in the matter; you have consigned your voice, opinion, and will. Countless people are *"committed"* to their girlfriend or boyfriend and suggest they don't need to marry because of such commitment. However, God doesn't call people in relationship with Him to *"commit"* but to *"surrender."*

Since human marriages reflect our relationship with Christ, we, too, must surrender ourselves to our spouse. There's no out this way because you aren't controlling the relationship—God and your spouse are. Commitments are broken at will every day because the one committed controls how long they remain. When both the husband and wife surrender to each other, there is an unbreakable force, yet in today's marriages, both want to do nothing more than commit so that they can leave if they eventually want out.

When we say marital vows, most miss they are supposed to be a form of surrender, a giving yourself to the other; two becoming one—both are surrendered making one new creation. Because people miss this, too many are committed for a season, but eventually check out with legal divorce or emotionally though remaining married. In living together unmarried, one inadvertently surrenders to a person sans covenant, which can only lead to a disaster. This is why people living together, having taken each other's bills, kids, property, etc., feel trapped though they're actually free to leave. Surrender means crucifying self; it means to lay down your life for another. We all need to stop surrendering ourselves to one without covenant because, without covenant, there is no protection, and all the lines of right and wrong are blurred, leaving everyone confused and imprisoned.

To reiterate, God doesn't call anyone to "*happiness*," but "*holiness*," just as He doesn't call us to "*commit*" but to "*surrender.*" Surrender causes one to become lost in Christ. Surrender causes one to become lost in their spouse. Surrender takes your focus off personal happiness [selfishness] and diverts it toward holiness [selflessness]. Keeping this in mind will assist you in the quest for the correct union of marriage preordained by God. Instead of asking, "*Will this make me happy?*" always ask, "*Can I surrender to them? Should I surrender to them? Can I utterly subject myself to them and be in right standing with God?*" These questions can save you from entering an unholy relationship of fornication, adultery, or unholy marriage and even save you from exiting a valid marriage gone sour.

Commitment and happiness = self-focus and personal control
Surrender and holiness = God-focus and control abandonment

Prayer of Purity:

Father, may I be self-controlled as Jesus was when He walked in human flesh. As I seek purity, reveal to me the weaknesses of my flesh that I will flee evil instead of deceiving myself into thinking I have strength I do not possess. Lead me into the path of righteousness that I will not cast my foot upon a stone and stumble and fall. I choose today to crucify my fleshly man and receive Holy Spirit to take His rightful position as the ruler of my heart. I repent of all impure activity in my past and receive your forgiveness. I choose to abstain from all sexual impurity. Thank You, Jesus, for paving the way for holiness. Amen.

Notes

CHAPTER 6

Covenant Vows

What Man Brought Together:

> "What therefore God has joined together, let no man separate (Mark 10:9)."

The above text is often misquoted when trying to save marriages, so it is grossly misused. I implore us all to look at the wording—what *"God"* has brought together. In all my counseling those considering marriage or divorce, my first question is, *"Did God ordain* [bring together] *this union, or is it a manifestation of what man brought together?*

Unfortunately for everyone involved, the vast majority are brought together by man, not God. Even when two people are Christ-followers, it doesn't mean God was anywhere in the vicinity of their decision to marry. Too often, we think, *"I should marry him or her because he or she is such a good Christian, and so am I."* Again, it sounds good in theory, but God is nowhere on their radar.

Magnitude of Vows:

> "When you make a vow to God, do not be late in paying it; for He takes no delight in fools. Pay what you vow (Ecclesiastes 5:4)!"

"Again, you have heard that the ancients were told, 'You shall not make false vows, but shall fulfill your vows to Yahweh.' But I say to you, make no oath at all, either by Heaven, for it is the throne of God, or by the Earth, for it is the footstool of His feet, or by Jerusalem, for it is the city of the Great King. Nor shall you make an oath by your head, for you cannot make one hair white or black. But let your statement be, 'Yes, yes' or 'No, no'; anything beyond these is of evil (Matthew 5:33-37).

All that said and understanding there are occasions where divorce is inevitable, we need to discuss divorce ramifications. When you marry before God and man, you are making solemn vows not to be taken lightly. They are not so easily broken merely with a divorce decree. Let's look at the subsequent passages concerning God's take on vows and how they impact us eternally.

God says we are to never enter vows lightly. Remember in Joshua 9 where the Gibeonites, knowing God had given their land to His people, were so afraid of being killed by Joshua that they pretended to be from a faraway land to make covenant with Joshua? Their actions were deceptive. In haste, Joshua made an unholy covenant with a people God had instructed him to wipe away. Because he did not seek the Lord before entering into treaty, the repercussions lasted generations. We do this when we marry someone and enter unholy covenant not constructed by God.

Note what Joshua actually did. God had moved mightily through this man, a man who loved Yahweh with all his heart. He obeyed God's commands. However, we are all flawed and subject to momentary lapses of sanity. Joshua allowed pride to take root. God had been so faithful letting him and his men overpower every enemy that, eventually, he seemed to think the power was his. Because of this erroneous thinking, he got himself and his people into a mess.

So the men of Israel took some of their provisions, and did not ask for the counsel of Yahweh. Joshua made peace with them and made a covenant with them, to let them live; and the leaders of the congregation swore an oath to them. It came about at the end of three days after they had made a covenant with them, that they heard that they were neighbors and that they were living within their land…but all the leaders said to the whole congregation, "We have sworn to them by Yahweh, the God of Israel, and now we cannot touch them. This we will do to them, even let them live, so that wrath will not be upon us for the oath which we swore to them."…then Joshua called for them and spoke to them, saying, "Why have you deceived us, saying, 'We are very far from you,' when you are living within our land? Now therefore, you are cursed, and you shall never cease being slaves, both hewers of wood and drawers of water for the house of my God (Joshua 9:14-16, 19-20, 22-23)."

It's incredible how quickly Joshua blamed them as though he did nothing wrong. If he had only sought Yahweh as he had done every other time, he would have known supernaturally that the people were acting deceptively. It's a common practice of the nature of the flesh that, no matter how much we love God, we blame others for our suffering and shame. The flesh never wants to be accountable for its own error. It is easier to point out and blame the wrongdoing of another. This is what transpires when marriages go awry; we blame God and our spouse, never considering our own culpability.

Even though the Gibeonites' punishment was to become slaves to the Israelites, the Israelites forever had to protect them because of the covenant they entered. In chapter 10, the Gibeonites cried out to Joshua to come from Gilgal to protect them from the Amorites, and Joshua was obligated to go. God did, of course, take what Satan meant for evil and turn it for good (Romans 8:28).

Joshua understood the impact of a vow no matter how much he wanted to break it. Had he violated the vow, his victory at Gibeon would not have been what it came to be. Broken vows are a grave matter. God can turn it for good in the long run, but I implore us all to make the right decisions before entering any vow. Let's look further at Jephthah and the ramifications of his hasty vow.

> Then the Spirit of Yahweh came on Jephthah. He crossed Gilead and Manasseh, passed through Mizpah of Gilead, and from there he advanced against the Ammonites. And Jephthah made a vow to Yahweh: "If you give the Ammonites into my hands, whatever comes out the door of my house to meet me when I return in triumph from the Ammonites will be Yahweh's, and I will sacrifice it as a burnt offering." Then Jephthah went over to fight the Ammonites, and Yahweh gave them into his hands…when Jephthah returned to his home in Mizpah, who should come out to meet him but his daughter…she was an only child. Except for her he had neither son nor daughter. When he saw her, he tore his clothes and cried, "Oh no, my daughter! You have brought me down and I am devastated. I have made a vow to Yahweh that I cannot break." "My father," she replied, "you have given your word to Yahweh. Do to me just as you promised, now that Yahweh has avenged you of your enemies, the Ammonites. But grant me this one request," she said. "Give me two months to roam the hills and weep with my friends, because I will never marry." "You may go," he said. And he let her go for two months. She and her friends went into the hills and wept because she would never marry. After the two months, she returned to her father, and he did to her as he had vowed. And she was a virgin. From this comes the Israelite tradition that each year the young women of Israel go out for four days to commemorate the daughter of Jephthah the Gileadite (Judges 11:29-40).

All I can say to this situation is, *"WOW!"* It's interesting to me that Jephthah's response when he saw her was, *"You have brought me down..."* as if somehow his foolish vow was his daughter's fault; he did much like Joshua. In this case, the daughter was innocent, unlike the Gibeonites. I must point out something often overlooked. The daughter must have been very close to God, given her response to her imminent death. She did not go into a panic, nor did she come against her father or his foolish vow. She showed respect to her father and God; her concern was Yahweh and the vow made to Him.

Furthermore, look at her odd request. She did not want to go for two months with her friends to *"party,"* nor did she want to go to grieve her upcoming fiery death. She simply wanted to spend two months with her friends to mourn her stolen opportunity to marry. This is odd to me. Because we know she must have understood God and the intense value God puts on a vow, she equally understood the beauty and value of marriage—holy matrimony.

Prayer:

Father, I come before You in the name of Your holy Son, Jesus. Father, teach me Your ways, O Lord, that I will be slow to speak and quick to listen. Place a watch over my mouth that I may not sin against You. Stir discernment within me that I hear Your direction before making a wrong vow internally or externally. I bless You, O Lord, that You make every curse in my life a blessing through my love for You. I trust that eventually, all things work for good for those who love You. I vow my love for You so that I will walk a life of blessings in the Kingdom of God instead of curses set against the Kingdom of God. May the words of my mouth and the meditation of my heart be pleasing in Your sight. Amen.

Notes

CHAPTER 7

———— ❁ ————

What God has Joined Together

"What therefore God has joined together, let no man separate (Mark 10:9)."

Then Yahweh God said, "It is not good for the man to be alone; I will make him a helper suitable for him." Out of the ground Yahweh God formed every beast…but for Adam there was not found a helper suitable for him. So Yahweh God caused a deep sleep to fall upon the man, and he slept; then He took one of his ribs and closed up the flesh at that place. Yahweh God fashioned into a woman the rib which He had taken from the man, and brought her to the man. The man said, "This is now bone of my bones, and flesh of my flesh; she shall be called Woman, because she was taken out of Man." For this reason a man shall leave his father and his mother, and be joined to his wife; and they shall become one flesh (Genesis 2:18-24).

The content of this chapter will overlap with chapter six. Still, I believe we must notice several vital things in the above Scriptures as they have everything to do with being equally or unequally yoked.

What God has Joined Together:

First and foremost, it reads, "*What God* has joined together…" If no other Scripture indicates that God does ordain specific marriages, this one does. I have heard many say that the Bible does not clearly indicate that God ordains, creates, or chooses a mate one for another. Clearly, if God knows and places the exact number of hairs on our heads, surely He would put even more consideration into which person we marry, whether we choose correctly or not.

Also, in Genesis 2, I find it intriguing that God states He took a rib out of Adam to put into Eve. Although, obviously, she too came from the ground, the difference between her and the other created beings is that she is forever linked physically and spiritually to Adam, Eve's life mate. God created Adam from the ground without taking anything from another creation, and He could have created Eve without taking anything from Adam, yet He did.

It is my estimation that God did this to emphasize the value and validity of "*oneness.*" This happened in their situation physically and spiritually. In like manner, this is how we are linked together as one in current-day marriages. Physically, we are joined together through sexual intercourse, spending our lives together eating, drinking, making memories, etc. Spiritually, we are connected through verbal vows made before God and man. As we just discussed, vows are sacred to God; they are meant to be permanent, binding, lasting.

To recap, God says we are never to make a vow haphazardly. Numbers 30:2 reads, "*If a man makes a vow to Yahweh, or takes an oath to bind himself with a binding obligation, he shall not violate his word; he shall do according to all that proceeds out of his mouth.*" Again in Deuteronomy 23:21, we see it written, "*When you make a vow to Yahweh your God, you shall not delay to pay it, for it would be sin in you, and Yahweh, your God, will indeed require it of you.*"

These apply to marriage vows, business vows, flippant, sarcastic vows; any and all vows are a serious thing. I am reminded of Jacob and his haphazard vow to Laban in Genesis 31, which reads, "*Then*

Jacob replied to Laban, '…The one with whom you find your gods shall not live; in the presence of our kinsmen, point out what is yours among my belongings and take it for yourself.' For Jacob did not know that Rachel [his most cherished and beloved wife] *had stolen them.*" Later we see in Genesis 35, Rachel dies, giving birth to Benjamin. The vow he foolishly made in haste had to be honored.

Is Divorce Lawful?

Let's look at the following passage in Matthew where the Pharisees came to test Jesus:

> Some Pharisees came to Jesus, testing Him and asking, "Is it lawful for a man to divorce his wife for any reason at all?" And He answered and said, 'Have you not read that He who created them from the beginning made them male and female, and said, 'For this reason a man shall leave his father and mother and be joined to his wife, and the two shall become one flesh'? "So they are no longer two, but one flesh, what therefore God has joined together, let no man separate. " They said to Him, "Why then did Moses command to give her a certificate of divorce and send her away?" He said to them, "Because of your hardness of heart Moses permitted you to divorce your wives; but from the beginning it has not been this way. And I say to you, whoever divorces his wife, except for immorality, and marries another woman commits adultery." The disciples said to Him, "If the relationship of the man with his wife is like this, it is better not to marry." But He said to them, "Not all men can accept this statement, but only those to whom it has been given. For there are eunuchs who were born that way from their mother's womb; and there are eunuchs who were made eunuchs by men; and there are also eunuchs who made themselves eunuchs for the

sake of the Kingdom of Heaven. He who is able to accept
this, let him accept it (Matthew 19:3-12)."

We must address the line where Jesus said, *"Because of your hardness
of heart, Moses permitted you to divorce your wives, but from the beginning, it
has not been this way."* It was not that way in the beginning because
the initial marriage was between Adam and Eve—a marriage created by God. It is because our hearts have become hardened toward
God, or rather, against the perfect will of God, that disobedience
abounds, and unholy marital covenants abound all the more. Notice
this is where the Lord interjected the concept of being a eunuch.

Obedience to God would be praying for the ordained mate,
obeying God, no sex before marriage, not dating anyone you desire
just because you can, be patient with God, expectantly believe that
God has a better plan for you than whatever you could concoct,
and, above all, seek first His Kingdom and His righteousness (Matthew 6) trusting His ways above your own.

Does He or Doesn't He Choose Our Mates?

I was just reading where a minister posed a question, *"There are those
who believe that God chooses your mate for you and those who believe that the
male is responsible for choosing his mate. Let me hear from you? What do you
believe? Give Scripture if possible, please."* Many people weighed in. The
majority believed that man chooses his mate because God gives us
free will; God does not create a mate for people.

I believe 100% given all of the good and bad marriages of the
Old Testament all the way to current day, including my own personal knowledge from my life experiences, that God does not *"choose"* a
wife for man, but He does *"create"* one just as He did for Adam.
It was up to Adam to choose Eve or not. Isaac, Jacob, Boaz, and
others had women created for them and were directed to them
supernaturally, but they still had to choose Gods will or their own.
These God-ordained unions honored Him when they sought His

will through prayer. This is the root purpose of everything God plans—to honor Him. Hosea, the prophet, was explicitly instructed who to marry and why.

There is no mate for those who are set aside as eunuchs by birth. For those who chose to be a eunuch or were made so by the hands of men, God already knew this in advance, before the foundation of the Earth. I don't understand strong people of God believing that an all-knowing God would say, "*Here you go. Here are a bunch of people—pick one that you like*" or "*Oops, I didn't know you were a eunuch, so I accidentally created a mate for you. I guess the mate is just out luck and on their own!*" I ask with sincerity, does that make any sense? Many make themselves eunuchs because their ordained mate married the wrong person leaving them no choice but to be celibate. One wrong marital choice throws God's perfection way off course.

Every God ordained marriage in the Old Testament was preordained. It means that God strategically planned the union with great thought and detail before the foundation of the Earth. That is why the marriages were successful even though the people themselves were flawed. We do have the God-given right to choose anyone we want, just as we all have the right to choose Jesus or not. Thats part of free will. Just because someone doesn't choose Jesus, does that mean there is another way to God the Father? No. It is radically and painfully apparent to all that mankind has, generally speaking, chosen poorly in all areas of decision making, including choosing marital mates.

For those who purpose to ultimately seek God's face, hear His heart for their purpose, listen to His bidding, choose patience in all matters, and trust His perfect timing, are brought together with the mate God created just for them. We see so much divorce and tragic marriages within the body of Christ, including within the leadership, because we pick according to our standards, wants, likes, and dislikes choosing not to wait upon Yeshua.

Marriage on Earth reflects our spiritual marriage to God—unfortunately, they are a disgraceful display at best. We make such poor choices because we say with our lips, *"I love God,"* yet we don't trust Him enough to wait for Him to bring into our lives that which He orchestrated. We don't generally have enough faith to believe God is big enough or thoughtful enough to create someone for us or us for someone. Instead, we do our own thing because it may have the appearance of holiness yet is altogether unholy. Worse, not only are our choices in a spouse not for us, but they are against us, and we want God to fix our unholy covenant He never purposed from the start.

God is so intricate in His planning and timing that He creates a mate to marry. That is why the Word reads, *"What God has brought together."* Old Testament to current day, unholy covenants have taken place at the hand of our foolish choices and will proceed well into the future. We are led by emotions, hormones, loneliness, even— and especially—within the body of Christ. Therefore, Holy Spirit had no say in the matter. Now, having new knowledge of our own personal missteps, dare we question God why our marriage is so horrific?

We all know and can quote, *"'For I know the plans that I have for you,' declares Yahweh, 'plans for welfare and not for calamity to give you a future and a hope* (Jeremiah 29:11).»* I wonder if we recognize and readily accept a plan for every minute area of every person's life. God is orderly knowing His plans for us. If we don't seek His face, we miss it and make our own plan as we go along; we usher our own demise, no fault of God. Few wait upon the Lord due to foolish fleshly desires not reigned into obedience to Christ.

Since two become one, would God so sloppily not create two specific people for one another? We conduct ourselves as if God is saying, *«Yes, two become one, which is a solemn thing, but that isn't My problem. I left you abandoned without direction. Do whatever you want. However, you desire and don't even suggest that I [God] have time to bother with such things. Figure it out."*

In closing, remember that we become one entity in our marriage to Christ—completely losing ourselves in Him. In human marriage, two become one—both are to lose themselves in the other, creating one new entity. Is that not serious enough an issue for God to plan ahead? He ordains, but we choose.

> But I want you to be free from concern. One who is unmarried is concerned about the things of Yahweh, how he may please Yahweh; but one who is married is concerned about the things of the world, how he may please his wife, and his interests are divided. The woman who is unmarried, and the virgin, is concerned about the things of Yahweh, that she may be holy both in body and spirit; but one who is married is concerned about the things of the world, how she may please her husband (I Corinthians 7:32-34)."

Notes

_____

_____

_____

_____

_____

_____

_____

_____

_____

_____

_____

_____

_____

_____

_____

_____

CHAPTER 8

Two Halves Do Not Make a Whole

"Be ye not unequally yoked together with unbelievers: for what fellowship hath righteousness with unrighteousness? And what communion hath light with darkness?" (II Corinthians 6:14, KJV).

Unequally Yoked:

Right out of the gate, most everyone can quote the above Scripture, yet few really comprehend the depth of its meaning. For example, when I was growing up, I was taught that *"unequally yoked"* meant that no Independent Baptist should mix with any other type of Baptist—Southern, Free Will, etc. Definitely, we were not to intermarry with any other *"foreign"* denomination such as Lutheran, Methodist, and absolutely not with a Pentecostal or Presbyterian! Also, no person should ever mix with anyone outside their own race, nationality, political or social status. Then there is the actual reality that no follower of Christ should marry a non-follower of Christ.

In the Old Testament, God clearly instructed His people repeatedly that they were not to marry outside their race. What was

God's motivation in this command? Was He prejudiced against the skin color He created or against language He designed? No. God gave this command to keep His holy people pure of other gods, of worshipping anyone other than Himself. We must remember that the Old Testament is about things manifesting naturally. The New Testament is about something happening in the spiritual. The Old Testament always mentions external looks, yet the New Testament does not speak of outward appearance. The reason is because things in the natural come first, then the spiritual. Unequally yoked has nothing to do with anything external—it's spiritual.

I Corinthians 15:46-47 states, *"The first man, Adam, became a living soul. The last Adam became a life-giving spirit. However, the spiritual is not first, but the natural; then the spiritual."* In the grand scheme, the spiritual is first—God is Spirit. He has no beginning and no end, but this reference is written for the Earth, for mankind. We are physical man [natural first], but we can become spiritual through Holy Spirit [spiritual second]. It's all about keeping things within God's perspective and order.

Since God chose to exclude external appearance in the New Testament, we must pay attention and follow suit; He omitted it for a purpose. We are to owe no man anything but love. Money issues aside, it translates, *"All men owe every man love, regardless of anything external."* With that understanding, we can eliminate any false meaning for being unequally yoked having anything to do with outward appearance, especially skin color. As far as denominations are concerned, God is not a God of denomination but of a heart condition. If a black Baptist woman is in love with Christ, and a white Methodist man is in love with Christ, what should man do to hinder them from marrying? These have nothing to do with God.

To take this further, being *«equally yoked"* concerning holy matrimony boils down to one criterion—God's supernatural ordination. Nothing else matters. The problem lies in how we perceive *"equally"* or *"unequally"* yoked matter. Again, most people have an internal checklist they believe their spouse should meet to a tee, yet the list is generally not in compliance with God. Basically, we box God in so tightly that, no matter how clearly He reveals His will, we are too blinded by the flesh or religious and parental tradition to recognize. *"Do not judge according to appearance, but judge with righteous judgment,"* reads John 7:24.

Don't Judge by the Cover:

My husband is nothing like I pictured as a child. We must realize that when we first meet, our appointed spouses may be in no way ready for marriage, but that doesn't mean they never will. The issue is that often we meet our God-created mate but, since they are not on our mental checklist, we impatiently and foolishly marry the first person who comes along that fits our standard.

Cut two tennis balls in half, switch the halves and glue one half of one ball to a half of the other ball. Though they are the same exact shape, color, texture, and size, they will never make a whole; they are merely two mismatched halves stuck together. If you pour oil and water into the same bowl, just because they are together, for all intent and purposes, does it make them one new thing? No. It's just two vastly different substances cohabitating. The point is that just because two things appear as though they could mix, it doesn't mean they can, will, or should.

I fell head over heels in love with Michael when I was fifteen in August 1983, 10th grade algebra class, upstairs, A-hall, Mrs. Ward's class, at Lexington High School. This is the classic example of a good soul tie, but I was simply oblivious. I took one look at him, and that was all she wrote! I didn't understand it. I didn't know why. It wasn't based on looks, though he was handsome—it genuinely made no sense. It wasn't sexual, hormonal, emotional, or mental—it just was and with no logical explanation. Unfortunately, though we were algebra buddies and I helped him pass the class, we were but acquaintances. I wouldn't even call us *"friends."*

A few months after we met, he moved to another city an hour away with his family. I was devastated, to say the least. I remained forever in love with him nonetheless. I was friends with his female cousin before we meet. I would see him occasionally as he visited her. He later joined the army and moved overseas for several years. He met and fell in love with a young woman while abroad. As time passed, I eventually married someone else, and we moved overseas. My husband said he was called to be a preacher. Things *"appeared"* in order, godly. Though we married, the two of us never became one whole. He was an abuser. He did not hit me, but abuse comes in various forms. He was sexually, mentally, and emotionally abusive.

After separating from my first husband once back in America, Michael and I reconnected and became best friends. We could do so because he had moved back stateside, leaving his girlfriend behind. We remained friends with no romantic commitment or ties. Two years after my first husband left, I married the lovely, great guy I mentioned earlier, one who was handsome with a solid job and very kind. To my chagrin, we married one another—both on the rebound of failed relationships, which is always a formula for disaster. After two years trying to *"make it work,"* I left him. We tried several times to reconcile, but it simply was not right. We did not fit together to make a whole.

In 2000, after seven years of rebelling against God—beginning when my first husband left, I found myself on my face before the Almighty begging Him to show me the way to righteousness, purity, and wholeness. Though most of these stories are in my other books, my point here is that I finally submitted totally to God. I vowed I would never again lay with anyone, not my husband, or marry again unless and until it was as God intended from the beginning.

The blessings in Michael's and my lives are flowing for many reasons. The primary reason is that he and I make one whole person. We were designed one for the other. The first husband was like mixing oil and water, an apparent mismatch. The second was like those two tennis balls; we looked like a good fit but were altogether wrong. The third marriage is a perfect fit. God has blessed and blessed and continuously blesses without end. I took a vow of abstinence long before our engagement and wedding. Although he was reluctant, Michael complied.

Just because you are marrying your ordained spouse does not mean that the marriage will override sexual sin committed with that person; sex before marriage will hinder the fullness of God's blessings initially intended. Just because you marry the person within God's will, your poor conduct [fornication or adultery] before the marriage will taint the otherwise holy covenant. We must stay aligned with God before, during, and after marriage. Marrying your intended spouse does not give you permission to put the cart before the horse. It is altogether possible to ruin that which God intended to be pure. Our obedience in every aspect is crucial to receive the best God longs to bestow. It isn't that Yahweh can't or won't work around our sin once repentant, but why would anyone shortchange themselves? That would be much like Esau relinquishing his birthright for a one-time cup of soup!

God, in His infinite wisdom and love, created me for Michael. I thank God we finally came together as designed. If I had known at fifteen what I know now, I surely would have waited and prayed according to God's direction. I would have saved myself and everyone involved in those first two marriages a lot of heartache had I been wise as to how God ordains, not just the union of general marriage, but specific marriages. I never could explain my unwavering love for Michael back then, but now I can.

Please remember, I was a born-again Christian, and he was an agnostic when we first met. By man's standards, that would not be a union *"equally yoked,"* yet, it was altogether *"of God."* This is why we must tap into Holy Spirit as soon as possible and allow our spirit-man to become awakened to hear Holy Spirit speaking, leading, guiding. By no means could I have entered a covenant with him pre-Christ. However, when we allow God to reveal our mate to us, whether it makes sense to the common man or not, we will enable faith, patience, and grace to rule in our hearts.

This type of waiting takes knowing and trusting the absolutes of God. The more knowledgeable we become, the more consigned to Christ we become, the more faith we place upon Yahweh, hence the fewer mistakes we will make along the way.

Notes

CHAPTER 9

What about Love?

I wholeheartedly believe that once you truly love someone, you will never stop though the love will transition into a different type. Otherwise, if you cease loving someone, you never loved them in the first place. Love is everlasting no matter what transpires between two people, whether in marriage or friendship. Because genuine love is eternal, it can be tricky if we don't see and weigh it through the eye of The Way [Jesus]. Only when we view love from a Kingdom perspective will we correctly gauge relationships, the emotions thereof, and how to proceed in life.

Being twice divorced, I now have and will always have two extra men in the world I loved and made a covenant. Though I am divorced from both men, there will always be a bond on some level, no matter how much time and space between us. It's a fact no one can deny or remove. Because I genuinely loved both, love will remain unending, but the love is exclusively a supernatural agape love. It would behoove us all to seek for ex-spouses.

John W. Schoenheit defines the four types of love as follows:

> **EROS:** The Greek word for sexual love or passionate love is **eros**, and we get English words such as *"erotic."* When eros

was used as a proper noun, it referred to the Greek god of love. The Greek word eros does not appear in the biblical text, so we will not spend time on it in this article, but it has had such an impact on English and our view of sexual love that it is important to mention.

AGAPE: The Greek word that refers to the love of God, one of the kinds of love we are to have for people, is **agape**. Agape is the very nature of God, for God is love (1 John 4:7-12, 16b). The big key to understanding agape is to realize that it can be known from the action it prompts. In fact, we sometimes speak of the *"action model"* of agape love. People today are accustomed to thinking of love as a feeling, but that is not necessarily the case with agape love. Agape is love because of what it does, not because of how it feels—God so *"loved"* [agape] that He gave His Son. It did not feel good to God to do that, but it was the loving thing to do. Christ so loved [agape] that He gave His life. He did not want to die, but He loved, so he did what God required. A mother who loves a sick baby will stay up all night long caring for it, which is not something she wants to do, but is a true act of agape love.

The point is that agape love is not simply an impulse generated from feelings. Rather, agape love is an exercise of the will, a deliberate choice. This is why God can command us to love our enemies (Matt. 5:44; Exod. 23:1-5). He is not commanding us to *"have a good feeling"* for our enemies, but to act in a loving way toward them. Agape love is related to obedience and commitment, and not necessarily feeling and emotion. *"Loving"* someone is to obey God on another's behalf, seeking his or her long-term blessing and profit.

The way to know that we love [agape] God is that we keep His commandments. Jesus said, *"Whoever has My commands and obeys them, he is the one who loves Me…"* (John 14:21a). There are Christians who say they love God, but their lifestyle is contrary to God's will. These people mistake their feeling of affection for God for true agape love. Jesus made this clear, *"He who does not love Me will not obey My teaching…"* (John 14:24a)."

PHILEO: The third word for *"love"* we need to examine is **phileo**, which means *"to have a special interest in someone or something, frequently with focus on close association; have affection for, like, consider someone a friend."* It would probably be helpful if phileo were never translated *"love"* in the New Testament, because it refers to a strong liking or a strong friendship.

STORGE: The fourth Greek word we need to understand is **storge**, which is the love and affection that naturally occurs between parents and children, can exist between siblings, and exists between husbands and wives in a good marriage. It occurs in Romans 12:10 in the word *"philostorgos,"* which is a compound word made up of philos [the noun form of phileo] and storge. (end excerpt)

That said, we must decipher what to do with feelings of love. Forever I will love both my ex-husbands. Forever they will be a part of who I am because being with them through good and bad helped shape the person I am today. So the question remains, *"What do I do with the love I feel for my ex-spouses? If I love them, does that mean we should get back together?"*

As for my first ex-husband, mutual love appeared to RULE before our marriage, but it quickly shifted into hatred from him toward me, which ruled many years post-split. Eventually, because of his hatred against me, hatred formed in my heart against him. Once I came into forgiveness through Christ and began walking in agape love toward all mankind, I couldn't help but shift from hatred back into love. Regardless, it is not a storge love between a husband and a wife, but agape allowing my spirit-man to extend love where hatred would otherwise long to rule. With some folks, agape love can *"feel"* like love that would bring them to reunite in marriage. We must keep in mind that agape love is very different than storge, the love that would tie a husband to a wife.

Many divorced or almost divorced people come into Christ and assume that agape love absolutely dictates that they must reunite, and that simply is not so. This goes back to what I and many others have taught about not being led by the soul [mind, will, and emotions]. Just because you love someone does not mean you are meant to be together and that your love can sustain a marriage.

I dearly love and respect my second ex-husband, as I always have. My love for him is now and always was both phileo and agape. I married him because I misinterpreted my love for him as storge. Our marriage failed because of this misinterpretation, and many people were hurt, not excluding us two. Much guilt and shame on my part were involved in our divorce. My phileo love for him has never wavered, and it remains until this day. Phileo love does not mean we should remarry if we were both single.

It is of the utmost importance in our walk with Christ to understand the different types of love and how to properly walk in them. We should not try to hide that we love our ex-spouses, nor should we misappropriate our love and attempt to remarry with the wrong love. With a divorce, there is often a feeling of *"because I love* [agape or phileo] *them, I don't love my new spouse completely"* or *"maybe I am still in love* [storge] *with them"* or *"I have such strong love* [eros] *love for them, maybe we should have an affair and see where it goes."* All of this thinking leads one to a perpetual life of misery, pain, and guilt—often shame and remorse. God wants His people to live in peace, so much so that He instructs us to pursue peace voraciously!

Once you have moved on in life and, through seeking God's will, concluded your divorce is for the betterment of all, learn to love with agape love and leave the rest behind. If neither of you has remarried and you are both continually drawn to one another, reuniting may very well be the correct course. No matter what, and above all else, your relationship with Jesus needs to be your first priority. When He is your all-in-all, your relationships in this life will work themselves out in time. Jumping into or back into any human relationship is always going to be disastrous eventually if you do not first seek the Kingdom of God, His righteousness, His will, and His plan for you.

Prayer:

I desire, O God of Heaven and Earth, to walk in keen discernment to know how to love. I want to properly apply love as You have pre-ordained and not mix emotions with what is true and holy. I desire to keep myself pure in and out of marriage, no matter where I am in life. Reveal to me how to walk in self-discipline always. Selah.

Notes

CHAPTER 10

Understanding Adultery

"You shall not commit adultery (Exodus 20:14)."

Then the LORD GOD SAID, "IT IS NOT GOOD FOR THE MAN TO BE ALONE; I WILL MAKE HIM A HELPER SUITABLE FOR HIM." Out of the ground the LORD GOD FORMED EVERY BEAST OF THE FIELD AND EVERY BIRD OF THE SKY, AND BROUGHT THEM TO THE MAN TO SEE WHAT HE WOULD CALL THEM...BUT FOR ADAM THERE WAS NOT FOUND A HELPER SUITABLE FOR HIM. SO the LORD GOD CAUSED A DEEP SLEEP TO FALL UPON THE MAN, AND HE SLEPT; THEN HE TOOK ONE OF HIS RIBS AND CLOSED UP THE FLESH AT THAT PLACE. The LORD GOD FASHIONED INTO A WOMAN THE RIB WHICH HE HAD TAKEN FROM THE MAN, AND BROUGHT HER TO THE MAN. The man said, "This is now bone of my bones, and flesh of my flesh; she shall be called Woman, because she was taken out of Man." For this reason a man shall leave his father and his mother, and be joined to his wife; and they shall become one flesh. And the man and his wife were both naked and were not ashamed (Genesis 2:18-25).

Old Testament Adultery:

> "but I say to you that everyone who divorces his wife, except for the reason of unchastity, makes her commit adultery; and whoever marries a divorced woman commits adultery (Matthew 5:22)."

Definition of Adultery: being unfaithful to covenant vows in any capacity; spiritually, physically, mentally, emotionally, and financially; covenant betrayal

One of the treacheries against God we see so much in the Old Testament is adultery, otherwise noted as *"prostitution."* For obvious reasons, adultery here is not sexual—it is the total package of covenant betrayal. Many throw Matthew 5:22 at people concerning divorce stating that the only legal ground for divorce is adultery, yet we foolishly automatically think of adultery exclusively as sexual, much like we misuse intercourse assuming it's exclusively sexual in nature. This is where great confusion enters.

Adultery comes in many, many forms. It is, in short, unfaithfulness to the covenant vows of marriage; sexual misconduct is adultery, no doubt, but so are many other forms. We should not limit the broad spectrum of its definition lest we leave people in confusion and condemnation. We, God's people, are His bride. In Jeremiah 3:9, God referred to His people as committing *"whoredom...defiled...with stones and stocks."* Do we read about sexual misconduct? We do not.

In wedding vows, the promise between the groom and bride is to be faithful and loving always, committed fully to the other as long as they both shall live and forsake all others. However you slice it, to break these vows in any capacity—sexually, mentally, emotionally, physically, or spiritually, adultery has been committed. E.g., when a person places more value on their career, friends, hobbies, children, or anyone or anything else, adultery is committed. To be physically present in the marriage without another person involved, yet has pulled away mentally or emotionally, leaving the spouse lonely and abandoned is adultery, make no mistake.

Biblical Scope of Adultery:

To understand the full spectrum of *"adultery,"* we must realize that adultery is in full force when any of the covenant vows are forsaken. This is why so many struggle attempting to stay in a loveless, comfortless, honor-less, and lonely marriage. Most Christians are told, *"If the act of adultery* [sexual misconduct] *has not occurred, you have no grounds for divorce."* How many people forsake their bride or groom for work, friends, family, hobbies, etc.? To reiterate, the vows say, *"Forsaking all others, being faithful only to her or him so long as you both shall live."* So, adultery has clearly transpired when any of these vows in any form are broken.

I read an article by Robert Walters entitled, *The Biblical Definition and a Biblical Conclusion.* Here is a portion of that article it's well worth reading:

> The Bible is not a dictionary, thus we should not expect it to define a word in the same manner as would a dictionary. The Bible is the Word of God composed of various books and letters. In defining adultery, we must study and compare various passages of Scripture. This is the only way to ensure an accurate, scriptural definition.
>
> As is often the case, a word may have more than one definition. Some, for example, would say that adultery is nothing more than *"the act of sex a married person has with the spouse of another."* To believe this, one would have to be ignorant of or deliberately ignore a number of Scriptures that contradict such a definition. The Scriptures reveal that adultery is used to describe different actions committed by an individual or group. But the result is always an action contrary and detrimental to the covenant known as marriage.

The narrow definition of the word that some espouse is merely effort to defend traditional error. In defining adultery, consider the following Scriptures:

> And it came to pass through the lightness of her whoredom, that she defiled the land, and committed adultery with stones and with stocks (Jeremiah 3:9, KJV)."

This passage tells us that "*she*" [God's people] committed adultery with stones and stocks. These things were party to the sin. When we understand the sin, we will understand adultery as it relates to the present marriage, divorce, and remarriage controversy. A covenant was made between the nation of Israel and God. Israel agreed to abide by the terms of the covenant and God promised to bless them. The stones and stocks were the objects to which God's wife [Israel] gave its affections. The foreign object that adulterated the relationship served to replace God. God divorced Israel and the relationship He had with them ceased to exist. No sex was involved, yet adultery was committed! Therefore, if anyone tells you that "*adultery is nothing but a sex act*," you may want to refer him or her to the Scripture noted above.

Some, in an attempt to defend the traditional definition, may argue that adultery in the passage under study is spiritual adultery. But the sin in view here is marital adultery (Jeremiah 3:14), a sin that was an act of unfaithfulness to the marital vows, even though sex was not involved. Today, a person can commit adultery against his spouse in exactly the same way, without sex being involved. Virtually all admit that adultery is committed by "*putting away*" and remarrying (Matthew 19:9). Even those who are not capable of having sex are able to commit adultery in various ways, namely by simply being unfaithful to their spouse—acting as if the marriage does not exist and taking up with another.

> "And He said unto them, whosoever shall put away his wife, and marry another, commits adultery against her (Mark 10:11, KJV),"

This Scripture does not agree with the traditional definition of adultery. Jesus says that adultery is committed against the previous spouse rather than with the second woman he marries! We are compelled, therefore, to reject the traditional definition in favor of the biblical definition. This Scripture makes it clear that adultery includes the idea of the breaking of a covenant. But do not confuse the word *"breaking"* with the word *"destruction."* One may break the terms of a covenant; yet, if repentance and forgiveness follow, the covenant remains intact. A marriage is ended, destroyed, over, when one or both parties have legally declared the marriage to be over. The Jewish Law and the law of our land require a *"bill of divorcement"* or divorce certificate. When one who is divorced, and therefore *"unmarried,"* is unable to resist sexual temptations, he may marry another (1 Corinthians 7:8, 9). (end excerpt)

Is a Remarried Divorced Woman an Adulterer Forever?

> "All Scripture is inspired by God and profitable for teaching, for reproof, for correction, for training in righteousness (II Timothy 3:16)."

Or do you not know, brethren (for I am speaking to those who know the law), that the law has jurisdiction over a person as long as he lives? For the married woman is bound by law to her husband while he is living; but if her husband dies, she is released from the law concerning the husband. So then, if while her husband is living she is joined to another man, she shall be called an adulteress; but if her husband dies, she is free from the law, so that she is not an adulteress though she is joined to another man. Therefore, my brethren, you also were made to die to the Law through the body of Christ, so that you might be joined to another, to Him who was raised from the dead, in order that we might bear fruit for God. For while we were in the flesh, the sinful passions, which were aroused by the Law, were at work in the members of our body to bear fruit for death. But now we have been released from the Law, having died to that by which we were bound, so that we serve in newness of the Spirit and not in oldness of the letter. What shall we say then? Is the Law sin? May it never be! On the contrary, I would not have come to know sin except through the Law…but sin, taking opportunity through the commandment, produced in me coveting of every kind; for apart from the Law sin is dead. I was once alive apart from the Law; but when the commandment came, sin became alive and I died; and this commandment, which was to result in life, proved to result in death for me; for sin, taking an opportunity through the commandment, deceived me and through it killed me. So then, the Law is holy, and the commandment is holy and righteous and good. Therefore did that which is good become a cause of death for me? May it never be! Rather it was sin, in order that it might be shown to be sin by effecting my death through that which is good, so that through the commandment sin would become utterly sinful. For we know that the Law is spiritual, but I am of flesh, sold into bondage to sin. For what I am doing, I do not understand; for I am not practicing what I would like to do, but I am doing the very thing I hate. But if I do the very thing I do not want to do, I agree with the Law, confessing that the Law is good. So now, no longer am I the one doing it, but sin which dwells in me. For I know that nothing good dwells in me, that is, in my flesh; for the willing is present in me, but the doing of the good is not. For the good that I want, I do not do, but I practice the very evil that I do not want. But if I am doing the very thing I do not want, I am no longer the one doing it, but sin which dwells in me. I find then the principle that evil is present in me, the one who wants to do good. For I joyfully concur with the law of God in the inner man, but I see a different law in the members of my body, waging war against the law of my mind and making me a prisoner of the law of sin which is in my members. Wretched man that I am! Who will set me free from the body of this death? Thanks be to God through Jesus Christ our Lord! So then, on the one hand I myself with my mind am serving the law of God, but on the other, with my flesh the law of sin (Romans 7).

First, I notated II Timothy 3:16 simply to remind the general purpose for the Word. Secondly, in the very long text of Romans 7 above—none of which could be overlooked, we see that, by law, if a woman is divorced and the husband lives, the woman is considered an adulterer if she remarries. Countless women have struggled with this passage, stating that, according to this passage, any woman who is legally divorced and remarried is an adulterer forever lest her ex-husband dies—only then is she freed from the law. This seems cut and dry enough, but only if we read these texts absent from the remaining texts. Fortunately for us all, Paul did not stop with the first few verses!

This is where the importance of understanding covenant with God comes in, as written in chapter two. As the Word plainly directs, we see that the only way to enter into a valid covenant and be freed from the law is exclusively through death. The above reference begins with the physical death of the ex-husband as the only solution to the adulterous woman's freedom, but then Paul transitions quickly into the spiritual, diverting from that which is physical.

Remember that the Old Testament [Old Covenant] is physical, whereas the New Testament [New Covenant] is spiritual. What transpired back then [pre-Christ] did so physically, but what happens today [post-resurrection] is spiritual. To *"die to self"* is a spiritual term. In so *"dying to self,"* we are freed from the weight of the Law, and we enter into the rest and relief of the Law through Christ's Law fulfillment.

The Law reveals sin, and sin kills man. Sin kills man because no one can fulfill the law. Paul immediately instructs that we are all to enter into death, spiritually speaking, to enter the body of Christ. In so joining, death to the old earthly man has to occur. When death takes place, our new life in Christ frees us from the law—all the Law.

Bringing it full circle about divorce and adultery, we see that the divorced and remarried woman is an adulterer by law [earthly, old man]. However, Paul shifts attention to all sin—that all people are sinful—that the flesh [physical] of anyone [man or woman] is sinful. Once in Christ, divorced, single, or married, we are exempt from the law [physical], which binds our human form to the condemnation of adultery of any kind; the adultery of breaking the Law of our holy God.

In other words, though the Law condemns everyone in their *"adulterous condition"* against God, once in Christ, we are no longer a slave to sin. Therefore, we are no longer an adulterer. Too many people focus on the first section of *"an adulterous woman,"* citing that no woman can remarry if her first husband lives lest she is a whore. Yet, Paul's whole intent is not the physical adulterous woman but rather pointing to understanding adultery against God and how to become free from adultery forms.

In doing so, he points to us all as sinful in need of death [spiritually] to partake of the new life offered by God through Christ. If you are in Christ, and if you are divorced legally, and if you are lawfully remarried, you are not adulterous—you are free! Dying to self, as notated in chapter two, allows us to enter into the rest [peace] of Christ and, in turn, we are freed from the Law, which keeps us all under condemnation. You are free!

The "*I Stay for God*" Lie:

I know couples where one or both say, "*I only stay with you because of God; because He hates divorce.*" When I counsel people seeking divorce and I hear them quote, "*God hates divorce,*" I ask three questions:

1. Does God hate divorce more than He loves the people within the confines of the marriage?
2. Did God bring this union together, or did the flesh?
3. Was adultery committed?

Let's not forget that to commit marital adultery is simply to "*set your heart elsewhere.*" In other words, it is to break covenant vows. I am for marriage, but I am for the marriages ordained by God, not those God has not sanctioned. The bottom line is that the divorce rate is high because ungodly marriages are higher. I always warn people that divorce is tragic, painful, and grueling no matter what, but to stay bound to a person God has not set for you and you are consumed with misery, how is God honored?

It's so easy to stay in a loveless [adulterous] marriage based on "*God hates divorce, and I'm suffering for Jesus,*" but I see this mindset as self-glorifying. God is not honored by you simply following Law. Is our heart genuinely set on God or just not having to endure the shame of divorce? The way God is glorified in staying in a loveless marriage is when one can have their heart set on loving their spouse wholly, not simply possessing the appearance of obedience.

If someone gets divorced, then I direct them to purity and righteousness with a heart focused on God so as not to enter yet another ungodly marriage based on loneliness, sexual drive, finances, and so on. The person who says they're only *"staying for God"* deceives everyone. That marriage does not honor God, but it is a lie. How does a lie please or honor God?

Prayer:

Father, I humble myself before You today in repentance of all unholy, adulterous activity, not excluding what I have entertained in my mind. I recognize that pornography is adultery as much as physically engaging in sex outside of my marriage bed. I also acknowledge that forsaking any marriage vow is adultery, including putting my job or friends above my spouse. Father, I come before You and repent and seek to restore the error of my ways. Thank You for always giving grace in the face of my sinful state. May I never put anyone or anything above my spouse that I may always (for the man) love my wife as You love the church, and (for the woman) may I honor and respect my husband as the head of the household. May I constantly submit myself to my spouse in honor of You. Teach me the ways of righteousness. Show me the error of my ways that I may confess, repent, and be made whole, first with and in You, Jesus, and secondly with my spouse. Renew our marriage that we may honor You in all we say and do. May our marriage be the beautiful reflection of our marriage to Jesus. Amen.

Notes

CHAPTER 11

Soul Ties, the Spiritual Aspect

"For this reason a man shall leave his father and mother and shall be joined to his wife, and the two shall become one flesh (Ephesians 5:31)."

"…and the two shall become one flesh. What therefore God has joined together, let no man separate (Mark 10:8-9)."

"Or do you not know that the one who joins himself to a prostitute is one body with her? For He says, 'The two shall become one flesh' (I Corinthians 6:16)."

"…the soul of Jonathan was knit with the soul of David, and Jonathan loved him as his own soul (I Samuel 18:1)."

"If a man makes a vow to the Lord, or takes an oath to bind himself with a binding obligation, he shall not violate his word; he shall do according to all that proceeds out his mouth (Numbers 30:20)."

"Death and life are in the power of the tongue, and those who love it will eat its fruit (Proverbs 18:21)."

Evil Soul Ties:

Basically speaking, "*soul ties*" are vows or commitments made to a person, place, or thing; they are a spiritual issue as they take hold in the spirit-realm, the intangible world. The vows can be internal or external, through thoughts, words, or sexual relations of any kind. Our primary focus concerning marriage and divorce is evil soul ties. However, evil soul ties can be between children and parents, employees and employers, ex-boyfriends or ex-girlfriends, or with any person, people, or things that draw you in an unnatural, unholy way.

Any person belonging to Christ needs to take the time to break all evil soul ties between themselves and any and every person with whom they have ever had sexual relations, struck a verbal or unspoken vow, or anyone with whom they have had traumatic encounters, including parents, siblings, family, friends—anyone. About places, you may have made an inner vow of, "*I will always be attached to this place*"—possibly where you grew up or a place you've always wanted to live—rendering you unable to move forward. With an addiction, you may have made an inward or outward vow such as, "*I will always be an addict*," leaving you unable to be released from whatever the addiction. Again, it's anyone or anything that you are profoundly struggling to let go of and can't quite figure out the strangely strong pull. Never forget that life and death lay in the power of words you speak.

As you see in the texts above, you'll notice «*two become one*," whether in or out of marriage. In marriage, the soul tie is good, healthy, of God, providing the marriage itself is "*of God.*" Sexual, mental, or emotional soul ties between people in a romantic or sexual relationship are harmful, destructive, and unhealthy. They can form because of the oneness of sexual intercourse or even the private desire to be with someone that isn't interested.

In the case of Jonathan and David, there was no sexual relationship, but one of brotherhood. Jonathan valued David over his own father, King Saul. God set Jonathan in place with David to protect David, the rising God-anointed king to replace King Saul. We can have both good and evil soul ties with anyone, but sexual soul ties are the strongest due to *"oneness."*

For example, you may have a dear friend with healthy soul ties, but simultaneously, you can have co-existing evil soul ties that need breaking. Simply pray something like, *"Father, I command by the blood of Jesus that every evil soul tie between me and _____ be broken and that every holy soul tie is strengthened. I praise You, Father, that I am connected to other people exclusively in ways that are healthy for my spiritual growth, for Kingdom expansion, and in ways that will glorify Your holy name."*

About soul ties between you and past or current sexual partners, all evil soul ties must be severed to have nothing linking you to them in the spirit realm. When they remain unbroken, evil soul ties can cause great harm in your current or future marriage. Sexual soul ties are created as you link together in oneness through sexual intercourse. Think about it. If you *"become one,"* all of their and your demons, flaws, and issues merge, allowing them access to you even after your separation. This demonic activity can cause significant mental, emotional, spiritual, and even physical distress. But, because it is spiritual at the root, you cannot so readily put your finger on what keeps you bound.

You can enter into a holy relationship and marry, yet those soul ties with past sexual partners keep you from giving yourself entirely to your spouse. Though it may sound farfetched, it makes more sense than anything I've ever learned. A person must take aggressive measures by the authority Christ has given the Church to free themselves from past sexual bonds whether they were married or not, and definitely in the case of rape and molestation. If an evil soul tie is with an ex-spouse, those, too, need breaking more so because there was covenant. Just as a piece of paper decreeing marriage doesn't fully bond people's hearts together, likewise, a piece of paper decreeing divorce does not automatically release you from a soulish bond.

We must remember that everything is spiritual because we were created by a spirit being—Holy Spirit. Since we are created «*in His image*," it stands to reason that we must deal with the spiritual aspect of everything; it is far more relevant and substantial than the physical. I must admit, the first time I heard of "*soul ties*," it sounded crazy to my natural mind. Yet, in my spirit, it registered as truth. Though the effects may manifest physically, soul ties are a spiritual issue in so much as the source lies in the spirit realm.

Being twice divorced, I found it a relief to learn of soul ties, how they work, and most importantly, how to be released. The more I experienced internal results from breaking all evil soul ties with ex-spouses and even parents, friends, and enemies, I took it further and broke all corrupt soul ties between myself and Michael. I then asked God to increase and enhance the good soul ties between us. It is, as they say, a beautiful thing! For those who have ever been molested, raped, or defiled in any way, those encounters can, most assuredly, leave lingering soul ties – break those as well.

To reiterate, when you think of the meaning «*becoming one*," you'll recognize that whatever demonic activity your partner has, they merge with all demonic activity in your life. Therefore, once you separate, what's theirs is still yours. Because it is a spiritual issue, you may find yourself drawn to negative things you were not before your encounter with them. All of their spiritual mess became yours through the soul. We must take authority over such bondage to be set free. It does not just "*fall away*" because you "*walked away*." Notice the following two Scriptures.

> "I also say to you that you are Peter, and upon this rock, I will build My church; and the gates of Hades will not overpower it. I will give you the keys of the Kingdom of Heaven, and whatever you bind on Earth shall have been bound in Heaven, and whatever you loose on Earth shall have been loosed in Heaven (Matthew 16:18-19).»

"Christ redeemed us from the curse of the Law, having become a curse for us—for it is written, 'Cursed is everyone who hangs on a tree (Galatians 3:13).'"

In Matthew 16 and Galatians 3, we see that we have been redeemed from the curse of the Law through Christ's blood. Through His shed blood, we have been given power and authority. A giant misunderstanding of Christ-followers is that, because Christ bore the curse, we can just *"get saved from hell,"* and all will resolve itself. I was raised with such a mindset, and trouble ensued!

Yes, Christ bore the curse, and all who receive Him through repentance automatically receive a pardon from hell, but with the pardon, we, heirs of the Kingdom of Heaven, have been given power from on high. Additionally, when we walk in obedience to His commands, we obtain authority to use the power to the fullest.

This is where we are to take the power and authority of the blood that bore the curse of sin and the Law to break all evil soul ties we created knowingly or unknowingly. God gave power and authority to Jesus; Jesus, in turn, gave it to the body of Christ. As the body, we aren't to just stand around willy-nilly with the mindset, *"Well, it's in God's hands. Whatever happens, happens."* This is foolish thinking at best. God clearly made us kings and priests to subdue the Earth; we are ambassadors of The King. With this God-given position, we are to take authority over our lives.

In Matthew 16 above, we see the words, *"Whatever you bind on Earth, will be bound in Heaven. Whatever you loose on Earth will be loosed in Heaven."* This is specific instruction to take up the mantle of authority and build God's Kingdom. We should begin to do this first in our own lives before we can ever have authority to teach, lead, or build others. With this understanding, we are to take authority over all evil soul ties we have entered through sexual encounters and emotional and mental strongholds. It's pretty simple, really. It isn't some form of hocus-pocus or witchcraft spells—quite the opposite because that would be of Satan. All one needs to do is:

1. Repent of anything unholy, ungodly, or sinful conduct (i.e. sex outside of marriage, including in the mind and heart)
2. Receive Christ's forgiveness granted at the cross
3. Apply the blood shed for all

Prayer:

Father, I repent of my sin of engaging in sex outside of marriage in my mind and body. I receive the forgiveness You gave to me at the cross of Calvary. In the name of your Son, Jesus Christ, I command every evil sexual, mental, and emotional soul tie to be broken from myself and —name everyone you can remember—as far as the east is from the west. Father, I bless You that You will allow to remain only the good soul ties that You desire in my life. I take up the authority and power You have given through obedience to Your commands and apply it to every area of my life. Cleanse me from the inside out, in the name of Jesus. I thank You that no longer can the demonic spirits of perversion, greed, lust, (name your stronghold) have any dominion over my mind, soul, body or spirit. I choose to remove the leaven from myself and be holy as You are holy.

Notes

CHAPTER 12

Soul Ties, the Physical Aspect

Balance:

I am constantly telling people it is imperative to be balanced in all ways. We need to be sure not to deal with only one aspect of anything, but rather both the spiritual and physical sides of matters. So many people—non-Christian and Christian alike—tend to deal with the tangible and omit the intangible or vice-versa, and it is to our detriment every time. That said, I want to cover the mental and emotional issues that linger after divorce, which eventually lead to unhealthy physical connections.

More often than not, both men and women avoid dealing with these issues because it's either embarrassing [pride] or they simply deny there is a problem [pride]. Either way, it leaves us searching for relief in other people; hence, far too many *"rebound marriages"* full of misery and woe.

I have been a victim and have witnessed friends, acquaintances, and counselees who became victims of emotional and mental distress stemming from sexual partners outside marriage, divorce, and unstable marriages. If people would willingly recognize and accept that unmarried sexual partners, bad marriages, and worse divorces leave us battered, bruised, maimed, and emotionally and mentally fractured, we would more readily address the issues before entering another romantic relationship. It may not save people from rebound dating, but it would definitely rescue people from rebound marriages.

I freely use myself as a perfect example of what not to do. After my first husband left me, in addition to being crushed, depressed, embarrassed, and bitterly angry, I was determined to never be one of those—in my words then—»*pathetic divorcee's who pine away the days*." I set my cap on not doing the very thing I inevitably did. I told myself I was strong enough to handle the worst of situations, that I would not be a victim but a survivor. Looking back, all I see are the weak lyrics of some sappy country "*love gone wrong*" song. How foolish I was. After all, I didn't know anyone divorced combined with gained wisdom; or at least no one close enough to speak intimately to draw from their experience and wisdom.

My purpose in writing this book is to shed some light on the subject to give others what I never had—insight stemming from experience, wisdom, and revelation from God. Oh, that someone, anyone, would have taken me under their proverbial wing and guided me through Holy Spirit leading to save me from myself. If I had known my rebellion would cause so much destruction, I would have humbled myself before Almighty God, quieted my ranting about how God had obviously forsaken me, and listened before taking another step in any direction.

Ladies and gentlemen, God and God alone through His Holy Spirit is the One and Only Comforter, Healer, Restorer, Refresher, Reviver, and Life-giver. Only through our humility can we position ourselves to receive newness of life on any level, of any capacity. Divorce is death. Make no mistake. Only God can resurrect you in your inner man and make you a new creation.

There is no surviving divorce. There is only God-granted restoration or, better stated, resurrection and reconstruction. Without

His life, only death is brought from divorce into any other relationship one may enter. If we are functioning in a death mentality [crushed beneath the weight of divorce], it will cross into every other relationship, bar none. Self-will and determination do not heal the wounds of divorce or any other bad relationship.

Death results in decay. As I determined in my fleshly man to "*be strong*," I was still nothing more than "*weakness veiled*." I took all my pain and buried it so deeply within myself that I actually convinced myself I no longer had any. Unintentionally and unknowingly, I lied to others because I first lied to myself. It seemed logical in my imbalanced mind to find a "*good man to love me*" to make me forget all the madness I experienced with the first marriage and divorce. So long as I "*kept moving*," I wouldn't have time to stop and assess the damage left in the wake of my divorce. The results were:

- My second marital train wreck.
- Hurting an innocent bystander and his family.
- Hurting my family.
- Hurting myself.
- Annihilating my testimony for Christ.

I say again that divorce is death. Death leads to more death because death is all it can breed. "*Be of sober spirit, be on the alert; your adversary, the devil, prowls around like a roaring lion, seeking someone to devour,*" states I Peter 5:8. Although I was a Christian since the tender age of six, I did not know how to accomplish this instruction. I quickly became fodder for the enemy, Satan. First, by entering into an unholy covenant; secondly, by suffering divorce; and thirdly, by having no clue what to do with the remains. Everyone must have the insight to do self-analysis, whether married or divorced. God's people need wisdom, and the beginning of wisdom is the fear of Yahweh (Proverbs 9:10). The fear of Yahweh is to hate evil (Proverbs 8:13). "*Evil*" is defined further in that text as "*pride and arrogance, evil behavior and perverse speech.*"

In the aftermath of my first divorce, nowhere was any wisdom or God-fear, and it was quite a while before they kicked in after my second divorce. Without question, I was the polar opposite of what God required of me for success. I was foolish, prideful, arrogant, and evil personified without fear of the Lord. Unfortunately, people are rarely clear-headed in bad situations. I wanted revenge, though I knew revenge to be God's business. I wanted to reveal my first ex-husband for the coward, swindler, adulterer, pathological liar, pedophile, cheat, and much more, he really was—I wanted him to die a painful death! I was consumed with hatred, unforgiveness, sorrow, shame, fear, and bitterness; all the while, I knew in my brain that all those were against the perfect will of God, yet, I did nothing to remedy my errant ways. I didn't know how.

Too many within Christ's body are just as I once was – ignorant while sitting on the church pew. And what does the Word say in Hosea 4:6, "*My people are destroyed for lack of knowledge. Because you have rejected knowledge, I also will reject you from being My priest. Since you have forgotten the law of your God, I also will forget your children.*" It's high time that God's holy people become educated in the ways of Yeshua.

By "*educated,*" I don't mean just gaining information, but gaining knowledge combined with a heart for God, fearing the Almighty over pleasing the natural fleshly lusts. I am not saying that everyone needs to go to church more or become more active in church functions. I am saying that we need to seek God's face and heart before we do anything else. We need to know His heart and how He is for us, not against us. When we are hurting, unless we purpose to seek the Lord, the natural response is to fill the flesh with fleshly, tangible band-aids—anything and anyone that makes us feel better internally or externally in the moment.

If we stopped criticizing God for what a horrible thing He did to us and began accepting that we have made poor choices all on our own, healing would come more rapidly. This does not mean beating ourselves as if everything is our fault, but humbly taking responsibility for our part and leaving the rest to God. Admit we have been hurt and beaten, humiliated and abandoned, or whatever the issue; then take the next step and correct our wrongs as Holy Spirit directs.

Wait upon Yahweh to restore you before ever considering entering another relationship. Sex will not fix your heart. Money will not heal your heart. Busy stuff at work, home, church, or anywhere else will not fix your heart. Getting married again for the sake of pretense or security will not mend your broken, wounded heart. Surrendering all to Christ alone will.

My Evil Soul Ties:

My personal experiences with evil soul ties are many, but I'll only share a few. They were due to witchcraft [him] and ignorance [mine] with my first husband. I didn't realize, at that time, how deeply he was involved in witchcraft. Unless we know enough of the Word and how to properly apply it, we are easily trapped. He wanted to marry me for several reasons, but one is because I would not have pre-marital sex. Somehow, I became his conquest instead of someone he loved or was God-led to marry. As many young people do, he also wanted to get away from his parents. He saw me as his escape.

For me, I had made an inner vow to marry him based on, "*Because I'm so ugly, I had better marry him because no one else will ever have me.*" I knew in my gut he was wrong for me, but I married him anyway. He and I had broken up for nearly two years, but when I ran into him, I felt a powerful pull to him I can scarcely describe to this day. I didn't even like him as a person. I suspected him of being a liar from the word "*Go*," which led me to break away the first time. Yet, somehow, I quickly became entangled at a glance, and there had been no sexual anything between us. I see now it was an evil soul tie afoot. It was a draw I could not seem to resist, though I wanted to and knew I should. When I walked down the aisle to marry him, my stomach sank, knowing it was so very, very wrong. My dad even strongly urged me to turn around immediately as the bridesmaids were sauntering down the aisle before us.

The story of my second husband is very different. I had attended a wedding at a nearby Army base with a friend. I told her I would definitely meet my new husband there. Sure enough, at the reception, I walked right up to the chaplain, introduced myself, and proceeded telling him what kind of man I sought. He said, *"Oh, I have just the man for you!"* I gave him my contact information and went home. I carelessly vowed to my friend that very night, *"You wait and see. I'm going to marry the man with whom he connects me. It'll be a story for the ages!"*

When he called, we talked quite a while. In that conversation, I knew he was not for me based on likes and dislikes. Against my better judgment, I set a date. When he arrived at my door, he was an hour and a half late—always a bad sign for me. To add insult to injury, I said, *"What do you think?"* referencing our destination. His response to my quetion was, *"Well, I was hoping for a blonde, but you'll do."* Ummm, not a great start to say the very least! We proceeded as planned and had fun. When we returned home, we sat on the sofa and talked a long time. I told him I was tired of dating, and he said the same. I told him that we should agree right then and there to date exclusively; that if it worked out, great, but if not, no big deal. Sadly, he agreed.

Because he was such a nice guy, he met my checklist, and of course, because of the vow I foolishly made, we inevitably married after a brief break-up. Again, I knew he was not for me, no matter how nice and handsome he was. I was so lonely, and he was such a nice guy that, again, I reasoned that the only logical thing to do was to marry him. We had also lived together, and I was ashamed before God and man. I felt spiritually obligated to marry to get me *"off the hook"* of living in sin [sex outside of marriage]. Nowhere was God the lead, or even acknowledged. Nowhere did I seek God's holy will. That soul tie was so strong I could not see right from wrong. I even told my dad that I refused to say the vows because I wouldn't mean them. My dad refused to marry us if I didn't, so I spoke them. Even after our divorce, I was riddled with guilt, shame, and condemnation. It wasn't until years later that I came to understand the soulish pull that needed to be broken.

Since soul ties are spiritual and not physical, they are much harder to detect and break lest you know how and where to look. I have personally broken evil soul ties with everyone I've had sexual, emotional, or mental encounters, such as with friends—past and present—and family members. In addition, I asked YHWH to enhance every good soul tie.

I have broken all evil soul ties with my parents, sister, with anyone I perpetually needed to please, live up to their standard or even felt the need to compete with, be jealous of, or hate. Basically, when there is a solid negative pull between you and another person and you feel you just can't break free no matter how strong your will is to do so, go to war in the spirit realm by taking up the Sword of the Spirit and sever those ties!

Prayer:

Father, I come before You humbled, broken, even shattered. I ask that You reveal everything to me, both natural and supernatural, that needs to be addressed. Without You, I am nothing and I have nothing. As I am dead, I seek Your holy face to breathe Your Holy Life into me. Show me the way from darkness into the marvelous Light that is You. O Lord, restore, refresh and renew me. Grant me supernatural ability to withstand the wiles of the enemy attempting to lead me astray.

Notes

CHAPTER 13

Biblical Soul Ties

Since we just discussed soul ties and how to break the evil ones, I am compelled to spend some time reviewing biblical and personal examples to help bring them into clearer light. We previously discussed how Jonathan and David had a good soul tie saving David from sure destruction. God created such a strong soul tie as protection that he escaped his fierce enemy, Saul. This was obviously not a sexual soul tie. Hence, we better understand that soul ties can be between any people in any relationship.

Rebekah and Isaac:

We'll begin with Rebekah and Isaac in Genesis 24. They had a good soul tie created and blessed by God. We must note that Abraham instructed his servant to seek a wife for Isaac and how and where to do it. Abraham was a man who sought God's will. He ordered his servant to do likewise in his quest for the proper bride. The servant obeyed, set out on his journey to Laban's house, and prayed for success. God blessed Abraham's wishes through his servant's obedience. When Rebekah and Isaac met, there was a definite soul tie. I love how Rebekah moved *"quickly,"* as the Scriptures reference twice. She did not hesitate to do as the man requested. She did not delay, and she was very humble. Their connection was God-breathed and instantaneous.

Initially, Rebekah and Isaac were both people who sought God's will. In her barrenness, Isaac sought God's face, and God opened Rebekah's womb. As the twins struggled in her belly, Rebekah sought God for understanding. He answered telling her that the younger [Jacob] would rule the eldest [Esau]. As the years passed, we know that Esau sold his birthright to Jacob for a bowl of soup. This is where the evil soul ties entered.

Jacob and Esau:

In Genesis 25, we read that Isaac loved Esau and Rebekah loved Jacob. We see that these evil soul ties caused division within their home. Even though the Lord told Rebekah that the younger would rule the eldest, He did not instruct her to conduct herself deceptively. I think division had an open door because of the evil soul ties, both parents to the sons and the sons with one another. Instead of Rebekah discussing with Isaac why he should not give Esau the birthright since he forfeited it of his own free will, she devised a scheme. Because of the scheming, a poor example was set for the boys, further fuelling hatred between them. Imagine if they had the insight to sit as a family and work out their differences honestly, openly. Things would have been vastly different! Evil soul ties cause division, chaos, confusion, and ungodly behavior.

Jacob and Rachel:

Those evil soul ties led right into the next generation. In Genesis 29, Jacob's story begins to unfold even more. Jacob fled because of the wrath between him and his brother, Esau. He came upon Laban's home, his mother's brother. We see where he and Rachel formed a soul tie almost instantaneously. We are told she was very beautiful in face and form. He willingly worked to marry Rachel seven years, but

God did not say that was necessary. Deceptively, Laban gave him Leah, the less attractive older sister, to marry in place of Rebekah. He then worked another seven years for Rachel.

Nowhere in the Scriptures do we read anything like, *"And Jacob prayed and sought God for instruction for a wife,"* or *"Rachel sought God to know what she should do."* We do not encounter a time where Laban sought the Almighty. It appears there were bad soul ties led by fleshly lust between Rachel and Jacob. It is very possible that Rachel was his intended wife with an initial good soul tie from God, but they chose to act in the flesh, hence going about everything the wrong way.

To emphasize, evil soul ties leave one spiritually, emotionally, mentally, and/or physically paralyzed. Because it is a bond of the human mind, will, and emotions, any guidance from Holy Spirit is quenched and muted lest we specifically purpose to break those bonds through the blood of the Lamb. Because they were compelled to act according to the soul's desire, destruction followed.

Rachel and Leah:

We read that the sisters, Rachel and Leah, were fiercely jealous of one another. Leah was jealous of Jacob's love for Rachel, and Rachel was jealous of Leah's children. In addition, the trouble compounded because of the evil soul ties they all seemed to possess with one another—Jacob to his wives and the wives/sisters with each other. Each wife gave her maidservants to Jacob to bear children.

When Bilhah and Zilpah bore children to Jacob, both Rachel and Leah declared, *"Surely God has blessed and favored me!"* Funny thing, though, nowhere do we hear where God declared His blessings upon them. Everything these women and Jacob did was driven by the soul, not the Spirit of the Living God. Their declaration of «*blessing*» ended up being more and more of a problem to all involved as the years passed.

We all know that Jacob bore the twelve tribes of Judah and can reason that they were God's will. Absolutely, God could have produced the twelve tribes in a perfect way, vastly different than what transpired through four jealous, angry, sad women and a man who didn't bother to say, «No» to Laban or any of the women. Eleven of the twelve brothers were full of wickedness, as we see later when they set out to kill their brother, Joseph, in a jealous rage. Joseph was the only holy and acceptable son before God from beginning to end regardless of fleshly weaknesses. Where Isaac favored Esau, we see where Jacob favored Joseph, and exceeding jealousy grew like cancer. Of course, as previously mentioned—and will be discussed again, all things work for good for those who love YHWH, but what a difference it would make if we began recognizing soul ties for what they are and deal with them accordingly.

Dinah and Shechem:

> "And Jacob came to Shalem, a city of Shechem, which is in the land of Canaan...he bought a parcel of a field, where he had spread his tent, at the hand of the children of Hamor, Shechem's father, for an hundred pieces of money (Genesis 33:19-20)."

> "And when Shechem the son of Hamor the Hivite, prince of the country, saw her, he took her, and lay with her, and defiled her. And his soul clave unto Dinah the daughter of Jacob, and he loved the damsel, and spoke kindly unto the damsel (Genesis 34:2-3 KJV)."

Let us now look at Leah and Jacob's daughter, Dinah. We read in Genesis 34 where Dinah, of her own volition, went into a foreign, ungodly land [a city of Shechem in the land of Canaan] where she did not belong to seek the "*daughters of the land.*" In other words, her curiosity about how other women lived got the best of her.

Next, we read where Prince Shechem "*defiled*" her. Many people and other Bible versions translate "*defiled*" as "*raped*," but defiled isn't necessarily rape as it can mean many things. It states that he loved her and would go to any length to have her as his wife. I conclude that where the King James Version uses the word "*defiled*," it is about Shechem and Dinah having sex before marriage and being of different countries—he from the idol worshiping Hivites, and she from Judah, the land of God. Defilement came from not being married, and forbidden to intermarry.

Because Dinah let her curiosity take over, she rebelled by going somewhere she ought not, a godless land. This led her to an evil soul tie between Shechem and herself. That soul tie led to his imminent death and all the men of his country. Furthermore, all their women, children, and spoils were stolen. There is more to this story about which I elaborated in my book *Out of Obscurity: Helping Women Find the Kingdom Power and Purpose*. For the sake of this topic, we need to simply point out that evil soul ties hurt, not only the ones who possess them, but everyone around them.

Simeon and Levi, the leaders of the deception of circumcision, murder, and theft, were led by emotion and shame to kill and steal from the Hivites. More than likely, if we look deeply into the Scriptures, we'll clearly see evil soul ties between Dinah's brothers and Jacob. Imagine their hatred for their father, given that he never loved their mother. It just goes on and on, deeper and deeper, unchecked.

David and Solomon:

We can also look at soul ties between David and Solomon [David's son, David and Bathsheba [Uriah's wife and Solomon's mother], Ruth and Boaz, Ruth and Naomi, Samson and Delilah, and Adam and Eve. Some of these were good, and some were evil. These are all people with whom most of us are familiar, but we can't help wondering why these men and women of God were so drawn to their conduct, whether good or evil.

With David and Solomon, we know David committed adultery, murder and added lying to his indiscretions, all of it for the lust of one woman who belonged to an honorable, loyal man, [Uriah]. When we look down the road as Solomon became king in David's stead, we see Solomon repeating his father's cycles and greatly multiplied. Solomon was given wisdom above all others, yet he acted incomprehensibly. Solomon had one thousand wives and concubines! What would possess such a God-gifted man to destroy himself in such a way? Soul ties—issues that cannot be rectified in the natural and must be dealt with in the spiritual.

Something inside Solomon drove him to repeat his father's offenses and many times over. We may even speculate a bad soul tie between him and his mother, Bathsheba. Solomon laid with women just as his father did. Nowhere do we read that Bathsheba willingly engaged with David. The Bible reveals that David saw her, sent his servant to fetch her, and had sex with her. That sounds exactly like rape. David's poor conduct concerning women was passed to Solomon and his children. David planted the bad spiritual seed reaped in his children.

Ruth, Naomi, and Boaz:

Then there is Ruth, Naomi, and Boaz. Ruth bound herself to Naomi willingly with a spoken vow. They had a good soul tie. It was a bond stronger than flesh and blood. Because of Ruth's holy conduct through this soul tie, God blessed them both richly through Boaz, her kinsman-redeemer. The connection between Ruth and Boaz was so strong that Boaz loved her intensely. Because of their good soul tie and love, he revealed to Ruth there was a younger kinsman. He could have withheld this information, but he did not. He gave the younger kinsman the opportunity to take Ruth, yet he declined. Boaz was a man of honor and did right by his love for Ruth. That love far exceeded the natural man.

Adam and Eve:

Look at the first couple—Eve was created from and for Adam. They had everything at their disposal. Somewhere along the way, an evil soul tie developed. It's always intriguing when I read about Eve's sin. After she ate, Genesis 3:6 reveals, "...*she took of the fruit thereof, and did eat, and gave also unto her husband with her; and he did eat.*" She didn't even have to say, "*Eat.*" In fact, Eve didn't utter a word to convince him to sin against the Almighty who had given everything except that one tree. She simply handed it to him, and he followed her lead. Yikes! Adam asked no questions! What in the world was he thinking? Evil soul ties are more dangerous than we can fathom. Once we become aware, we can make a preemptive strike!

Prayer:

Father, I come before You humbled by Your majesty, grace, mercy, and compassion! I recognize and acknowledge evil soul ties between myself and _____. I take up the Sword of the Spirit, which is the Word of God, and sever them by the power and authority You granted me through the blood of Jesus. Thank You for enhancing every holy and pleasing soul tie in my life. I thank You in advance for the wisdom to recognize things of the spirit realm that are so much stronger than anything of the natural, and I thank You for the insight to apply the tools You've set before me this day. I bless You, Lord, for giving me eyes to see, ears to hear, and a mind to understand and comprehend the battle in the spirit realm. I choose to stop warring in the flesh and begin to take my struggle into the spirit realm. Selah.

Notes

CHAPTER 14

My Personal Nightmare

I wrote this chapter to allow people to see where I have gone wrong, understand the ramifications of my errors, and teach how to sever toxic patterns in their own lives. It is not to drudge up the past, slander those who have hurt me, or blame others. It is intended to glimpse my experiences to recognize how not listening to Holy Spirit's voice led me down a path I could never have imagined. I want to help people see how anyone can move forward when wholly submitted to Christ and that hearts can mend no matter how irreversible pain may seem in the moment. There's always hope.

Let's back up to March 18, 1989. I am standing in the back of the church on my daddy's arm, watching my bridesmaids walk ahead. All I could think was, *"Oh dear God. What am I doing?!"* My daddy turned to me as if he read my mind and said, *"You can turn back now. You don't have to do this."* Oh, that I would have listened to the Father's still small voice inside me and my daddy's less quiet voice!

For lack of a more appropriate term, my first marriage *"lasted"* four years with four miscarriages. I entered marriage with a man professing a calling on his life to be a pastor. I always wanted to marry a pastor, so I deduced he must be the one for me. Although there were rumors of his cheating months before the wedding, I married him anyway. Since I didn't know at that time how to hear—or rather, recognize—Holy Spirit's voice, I brushed aside the rumors and that nagging voice inside of me saying, *"This isn't right."* Although I did love my first husband, I was so insecure that I genuinely thought no one else would ever ask me to marry them. Simply stated, I felt myself so physically ugly that I'd never have another chance at love and marriage. This is an excellent example of a myriad of poor reasons causing people to enter into unholy covenant.

Our first three years of marriage consisted of countless affairs, pathological lies, and utter betrayal on his part. The second and third years were in Germany, far away from family. In between all that, I had four miscarriages. In our fourth year, he professed to be a changed man and was still called to ministry. I convinced myself he was sincere because I needed to believe him. Soon after, we were appointed as teen pastors in my stateside home church. To my remorse, rumors of infidelity swirled quickly. Lies, cheating, and more lies were all I had in my charade of a marriage. When I questioned him, he insisted he loved me and proceeded to make me feel as though I had taken leave of my senses by suggesting impropriety. It didn't matter that I caught him red-handed with a fourteen year old girl. He still attempted to explain it away as though it were nothing.

One night we had a massive blowout about his cheating and panting after underage girls. Upon returning home from work the next day, I found a note on the coffee table. He had packed his belongings and fled. This left me lost, scared, ashamed, and without a clue what to do next. This was not what I imagined for my life. Sadly, I honestly didn't have the first expectation, good or bad, when it came down to it. This is how naively I entered a covenant of such magnitude!

I began venting my frustrations and pain with colorful language and ways way out of my character as the «*good church girl.*» As I reached out to my church elders, I was surprised to realize that no one knew how to help me, not even the pastor. All I heard was,

"Give it to God. Go to church. Stay in church," along with a plethora of similar clichés. Though my heart had been ripped apart, that was all people could advise. No one offered any real assistance or spiritual guidance. Their poor responses left me embittered against people, especially Christians. I was exceedingly angry with God, to say the very least. I couldn't figure out how I could have been such a *"good girl"* and still have this happen. All that went through my head was, *"What was God thinking? Had He forgotten me?"* Sound familiar to anyone? I became the classic, *"Why me, God?"* victim.

I decided to go my own way. I decided it was time to try my own thing since God had made a mess of my life, but God was never far from my thoughts. I tried to ignore Him, but He just wouldn't get out my heart and head, not to mention my daddy's voice telling me what to do. This went on for an extended period, so I reasoned I needed to find a good man and marry him immediately. Brilliant, right? That would do the trick, or so I thought. In short, that's precisely what I did, as expressed in the previous chapter.

Seven months later and only two years since the first one left, I married the second time. Within months, we bought a house. About a month later, he moved to Saudi Arabia to work. I lived back and forth between the states and Saudi Arabia over two years and experienced numerous health issues, including two more miscarriages. Several issues required surgeries stateside. Through all the chaos, I became more and more disconnected from him and became unaffectionate. We tried to make it work, but I did not know who I was, what kind of person I was supposed or wanted to be, or how to be a wife to anyone. The marriage ended long before it started, just like the first marriage. Again, I entered covenant flippantly with no expectations at all.

After that, I really became a mess! I had not entirely *"cut loose"* after the first divorce, but I did after the second. I didn't know what to do with myself. Now that I was getting a second divorce, and it was entirely my fault, or so I had convinced myself, there was much more guilt and shame heaped upon my internal pile. My family wanted nothing to do with me for over a year. They were ashamed of me, and I was just too angry and undone for them to deal with. I had become utterly unrecognizable to myself and everyone who knew me any length of time. All but two of my friends abandoned me. I was a budding muralist living from art gig to art gig. When it was good, it was great. When it was terrible, there wasn't a cent to my name. The term "*starving artist*" rings a bell. I was lost on so many levels.

Ten months after I left, I desperately wanted my parents to accept me again and be in right standing with God—whatever that meant. I decided I should go back to my second husband. I didn't want to, but I thought it was the right thing according to the Bible. I called him and said something to the effect, "*I don't love you, I don't want to be married to you or anyone, but take me back because that's what God says to do.*" And so he did. October 1998, I returned to him just to leave him again the following December. The guilt, shame, and condemnation mounted in my exceedingly wearied head.

Please understand that I loved this man very dearly, just not as a wife should love a husband. The more I hurt him, the more I hurt myself and everyone in our lives. At the divorce hearing, I cried more than he. To save my life, I couldn't figure out my problem. People would ask, «*What's wrong with you?*" My response would always be, "*If I knew, I would fix it.*" I felt like I was losing my mind. I hated who I had become and was spiraling further and further out of control. I went from blaming everyone else to blaming myself for more than my share of the load. There seemed to be no end to the madness. At the lowest point, I even contemplated suicide. There seemed to be no relief. I cannot praise Yahweh enough for placing Helen Tanner Melcher [my long-time friend since grade school] in my life as she was the one who helped me regain clarity that suicide was not the solution.

To add fuel to the fire, in 1999, while going through the divorce with my second husband, my first ex-husband re-emerged. He wanted to reconcile. He confessed some of his evil ways and professed he was a changed man—again; that what he did to me regarding cheating had been done to him. He vowed his undying love for me. He said he had made a colossal mistake, and wanted me back. Ummm, as if my life wasn't confusing and chaotic enough, let's throw two ex-husbands in the mix. Talk about feeling like the woman at the well! I finally told him I could never believe a word from his lips and leave me alone.

After spending the entirety of my 20s marrying, divorcing, having miscarriages, and becoming entrenched with bitterness, anger, and depression, I cried out to God. In the privacy of my home, I had my first Holy Spirit experience; it was a result of many years reaching out to God for answers. That night, God revealed ever so gently that my sins were no less black than my first husband's. Although I always knew that, it was still oddly and surprisingly revelatory. I suppose that until that juncture, I could not comprehend it. Though my poor conduct seemed justifiable due to hurt inflicted upon me, it was still sin worthy of death.

Through tears and anguish, I began to earnestly receive forgiveness, repent of unforgiveness, and seek how to extend forgiveness to those who hurt me in any capacity. It has been a long journey from there to here but well worth every step. I have since not only forgiven my first ex-husband, but I have received Christ's forgiveness. Christ made way for me to both forgive and release it all when He rose from the dead.

Fast forward from 2000 to 2010, I was walking close to God, a published author, had done TV and radio spots, taught Bible studies in prisons and other places, preached sermons, and was a firm believer in forgiveness; I was eight years happily married to Michael, a mother of two daughters, and had put the past behind me. There's nothing like God revealing hidden junk in the most unusual, unexpected ways when you least expect it!

In the summer of 2010, I exercised at a local gym. As I'm doing sit-ups, I see none other than my first ex-husband sitting in a chair directly in front of me. He and his wife—Melissa, a gal I've known since elementary school—were there. She decided to join our small workout group and was super friendly. Weeks passed. Every time I would lay eyes on him or hear his voice, it was like I stepped right into Germany in the early 90s. Every evil, vile, wicked, hurtful, sinister memory of him came flooding back like a tsunami! When I would go home, I was conflicted about how I was to respond. I had never been in such a situation. I was a minister, yet didn't know the godly response. I genuinely did not know. With all God had accomplished in my life, I clearly needed a new lesson in this particular area.

I found myself in absolute turmoil, angry and irritated. Finally, at a workout's end, I attempted avoiding Melissa as I was already having a bad day, but there she was. As we began our conversation, to my dismay, I lost all self-control—the very thing I firmly teach others not to do. In a loud voice, I ranted something like, *"blah, blah, blah...and I am SICK of seeing,"* as my arm and pointing finger extended in his direction, *"my ex-husband every time I come here to relax and workout!"* Silence. I collected myself, realizing I was speaking to his wife, who adores him, and quickly recanted and apologized. I calmly told her I needed to leave the gym. I further stated, *"I bless you and your marriage, but where he was/is an angel to you, he was the devil incarnate to me."* A few other words were spoken, and I turned and left as gracefully as possible.

She wrote me a day or so later questioning my forgiveness, closure, and peace. I had undoubtedly asked it myself. I didn't know what was wrong with me. At the end of it all, God did, without question, reveal to me that there were some deeply hidden unresolved issues in my heart. Also, I learned how to *"flee iniquity"* on a brand new level! We do not, I repeat, do not need to force ourselves to hang around people we know will cause us pain and provoke us to ungodly behavior.

I liken it unto a recovering alcoholic and a bar. I would never say to someone, *"Well, you walk with God, and you're no longer a drunk-*

ard, so there's no reason you shouldn't be able to go into a bar and conduct yourself using total self-discipline. Where's your self-control?" How foolish that would be. On the contrary, if you know what tempts you, flee the element of temptation. For me, seeing my first ex-husband twice a week, every week, was a temptation to use unsavory language, entertain anger, and quite frankly, throw a punch! It was spiritually and physically unhealthy for me. After all was said and done, I resolved my newly discovered issues and entered a whole new level of liberty.

Fast-forward several years; I can genuinely say there are no ill feelings when I run into him, and I do. His parents and I were very close, and we spent quite a bit of time together prior to their deaths. When his father died in October 2012, upon his request, I sang at his funeral and helped with other issues. His mom and I remained close until she passed in January 2022. He was pretty ill at ease with my presence during the funeral proceedings. I actually had the rare God-opportunity to express to him: *"I am not here to hurt you. I love you in Christ."*

Later, a friend asked me, *"Did you mean what you said to him?"* My response to her: *"Absolutely not! The flesh in which I dwell will always hate his flesh. However, Christ in me did indeed mean those words because Christ loves him as He loves all mankind. What do fleshly feelings have to do with the life of Christ in me? I have no life outside of Christ."*

The lesson for me was beautiful and poignant. It reminded me in what would have otherwise been my *"worst-case scenario,"* no matter what the flesh desires, my flesh is dead and my only life is Christ. I could have easily called him to the mat on lies past and present. I could have effortlessly exposed him, but that would not please Yahweh. Love is always the center of God's will and, therefore, must be the center of mine. If Christ is my life, then only that of God should be allowed to come through me. No longer is vengeance my goal, but mercy. I am great friends with Melissa, now his second ex-wife.

Prayer:

Yeshua, I thank You for allowing me to learn from the mistakes of others so that I don't repeat bad behavior. May I be. a person so consecrated unto You that I don't make a move of any kind, especially in the arena of singleness or marriage, that would dishonor You or Your Kingdom in any capacity. Amen.

Notes

CHAPTER 15

Forgive and Forget

"Brethren, I do not regard myself as having laid hold of it yet; but one thing I do: forgetting what lies behind and reaching forward to what lies ahead, I press on toward the goal for the prize of the upward call of God in Christ Jesus (Philippians 3:13-14)."

"For if you forgive others for their transgressions, your Heavenly Father will also forgive you. But if you do not forgive others, then your Father will not forgive your transgressions (Matthew 6:14-15)."

Forgive and forget is an interesting topic for all people in any area of life. For anyone who has ever been hurt by divorce, infidelity, rape, lies, or abuse of any kind, forgiveness does not come easily for even the most devout believer, let alone forgetting. It is much easier to forgive the one who harmed someone else rather than the one who hurt you.

The above text is very misunderstood in that many people think we are to literally erase our memory bank. This is not what Paul is expressing. He is instructing us to take charge over our thought life. Memories will forever be a part of any human being lest they have amnesia. It becomes exceedingly frustrating to anyone trying to literally forget. The more they try, the more they remember with vivid clarity. In this, they give up trying and are overtaken by the memories.

Change Your Thinking:

> "Set your mind on the things above, not on the things that are on Earth (Colossians 3:2)."

We need to change our thinking to that of the Spirit of the living God instead of the Earth. I have written numerous times that we are to "*die to the flesh*" because the written Word of God clearly instructs this. By dying to the fleshly way of thinking, we can see through God's single vision. In doing so, we can see the greater good in all God is doing instead of just the bad circumstances happening to us. Forgetting after forgiveness is simply choosing to no longer focus your attention on that which once caused you pain and suffering. For that matter, stop focusing on a source that once caused great happiness, but has been removed.

Authentic forgiveness can come only when you are confronted with a real offense. If forgiveness comes easily, there was nothing so big an issue. Supernatural forgiveness can come only when the flesh would rather hold fast to unforgiveness. That's what makes it "*supernatural.*" Forgiveness is an act of agape love the other person does not deserve—it is sacrificial love.

In this, we set free ourselves and the offender. Many offended people don't forgive because they do not want the offender free. When we keep them in bondage, we keep ourselves there also, and more so. No one deserves God's forgiveness, so who are we to withhold forgiveness from the vilest offender? True love is sacrifice; forgiveness is true love, and it covers a multitude of sin.

Like I wrote before, when I returned to Christ, I was alone in my home crying out to God to show me the direction out of the overall mess in which I found myself. I heard Holy Spirit speak something like, *"You must stop viewing your ex-husband's sins against you as worse than any sin you have committed. You must forgive him."* I genuinely thought I had forgiven him years before, but forgiving in word is not the same as genuine forgiveness from the heart (Matthew 18:35).

I began weeping before the Lord in repentance for all I had held against my first ex-husband. At that time, I had not been taught that people need to forgive and repent of judgment against the offender. This is one of many things I love about Holy Spirit—when He teaches directly from His heart to yours, there's no need for a physical teacher or mediator. From that point forward, I began seeking the heart and face of God on a level I had never known. I began to hunger and thirst for Christ as I had never known, and I certainly didn't understand.

Looking back, I can see that the more I sought Yeshuah's face, the less vivid my painful memories became. The more I discovered His heart, the less I concerned myself with holding on to the evil set against me. The more I learned God and His ways—not just *"about"* God, but His heart, the more I understood how I had allowed myself to make such drastically wrong choices. I could no longer blame others for their sins against me. I was at a place of personal accountability as well as personal transformation. I became positioned to receive Christ's forgiveness as much as I could forgive others. The more I forgave and repented judgment against others, the more freedom I experienced.

Let's analyze the words of Paul in Philippians 3, *«I do not regard myself as having laid hold of it yet; but…."* The first part of his words confesses he does not have it all perfect, not yet. We are all a work in progress. It would be phenomenal to suddenly have revelation from God and instantly become perfect in all ways, but that is not the case for anyone, no exclusions. Knowing this should bring us comfort and the leeway to cut ourselves some slack when we falter.

Forgiveness Instructions:

The next section of his words is, "*...one thing I do: forgetting what lies behind and reaching forward to what lies ahead....*" First, he tells us of one thing he does. This lets us know that it is not exclusive, but one of many things; he takes other actions in addition. The thing he does is twofold: forgetting and looking toward the future. Please note he doesn't merely "*forget*" as in memory loss, but he "*forgets*" by changing his focus. Throughout the Bible, God instructs His people to:

1. Focus on whatever is true, honorable, right, pure, lovely, of good repute, excellent, and that which is worthy of praise, dwell on these things (Philippians 4:8). This means we have a choice about what we think.
2. Set our minds on things above instead of the things of the Earth, e.g., bad memories, good memories that no longer exist, people you miss and long for, etc. (Colossians 3:2). Again, it's all about what we choose to ponder.
3. Accept that we are raised and seated with Him in the heavenly places in Christ Jesus (Ephesians 2:6). He insists that we know our Christ-position. When we know that position, we can focus on the unseen and the broader perspective—present and future—rather than the here-and-now life issues. In other words, we will stop making snap emotional decisions based on the circumstances, and start looking at the bigger picture and possible repercussions in the future. Our Christ-position causes us to pause, pray, ponder, and then respond.
4. Meditate on His Word day and night without ceasing (Psalm 1). Here we are again—He implores us to choose to focus on His Word over anything of this world.

5. Know the promises in Christ (II Peter 1:4). When we know the promises, we can stand firmly in them, anticipating His fulfillment. Our atmosphere will shift when we focus on promises instead of problems.

6. Seek first the Kingdom of God and His righteousness, and all we need will be given (Matthew 6:33). We must decide what we want to seek: old memories or God's Kingdom. The choice belongs to us alone.

7. We must take authority over our thoughts (I Corinthians 10:5-6)! We have the authority to pull down everything that comes into our minds. We do not have to allow anything to stay in our mind we don't want, or instead, what God does not want.

There are so many more than these seven listed, but it's a small taste of how to forgive and forget. Forgiving comes from understanding that no one needs grace and mercy any more or less than another. When we realize Christ buried not just our acts of sin [plural] but our sinful nature [singular], we'll better understand that He died for all because all need a blood transfusion. Without it, we are doomed, whether we sinned only once or whether we lived a life of perpetual sin. Acts of sin are merely an offshoot of the sin nature; hence, the acts are not God's concern, but rather the tainted blood of Adam running through mankind's veins.

Freedom Tool:

When Holy Spirit instructed me to forgive my ex-husband, it changed everything. I finally realized that my sins were no less vile than his against me. I was utterly humbled before a most holy God. It's when we allow pride [the root of all evil and prejudice] to remain that we play the comparison game. When we play this game, we deceive ourselves into thinking we are justified in our unforgiveness and judgment. When we justify our unforgiveness and judgment against our offender, we hurt our relationship with Christ—we destroy ourselves by our own hand. It is foolishness at its finest.

When, however, I accepted that my sin nature is no less tainted than the one who harmed me, forgiveness came with much greater ease. When I realized that holding judgment in my heart against my offender, I endangered my own life—the very life I struggle to keep healthy and whole. When I chose to set my mind on God—His greatness, majesty, mercy, and grace—I ceased thinking about how much I hated and despised someone. The pain began to diminish. The anguish started to seem small in the face of such an awesome God. How much more should we forgive our perpetrators if God can forgive our sinful nature?

In light of God's heavenly perspective, forgiveness is the most fantastic freedom tool He could ever grant. Simply stated, forgiveness is an act of humility and God-love because authentic forgiveness is foreign to the natural man. It is an act of God's supernatural realm, from the One who is Love. Repenting judgment against someone in light of God's heavenly perspective is the greatest asset in keeping ourselves from doing the very thing we hate in someone else. Below are a few vital Scriptures concerning forgiveness and judgment.

> "You have no excuse, you who pass judgment on someone else, for at whatever point you judge the other, you are condemning yourself, because you who pass judgment do the same things (Romans 2:1)."

> "For if you forgive others for their transgressions, your Heavenly Father will also forgive you. But if you do not forgive others, then your Father will not forgive your transgressions (Matthew 6:14-15)."

> "There is no fear in love; but perfect love casts out fear, because fear involves punishment, and the one who fears is not perfected in love. We love, because he first loved us (1 John 4:18-19)."

Unforgiveness and harbored judgment are a downfall. Hebrews 12:15 reads *"See to it that no one misses the grace of God and that no bitter root grows up to cause trouble and defile many."* Resentment, as mentioned in Job 36:21, is the equivalent of godlessness. I challenge you to dig deeply into your past and inspect your heart. Only God can reveal to you the genuine condition of your heart. Seek Him to expose all roots of bitterness, unforgiveness, and judgment that have been allowed to take hold and defile, not only you, but family and other relationships in your life. As hard as this may be, the outcome is far superior to your current condition.

Many do not realize that forgiveness and repentance of harbored judgment are for self, not the offender. Many also think they need to go to every person against whom they have held unforgiveness to judgment and tell them everything. This generally causes more harm than good. It only stirs more dissension, causing greater internal and external conflict to yourself and the other party. When we isolate internal issues and our dealings with them, Satan has much less opportunity to take our good intentions and use them for evil. Too often, when we set out to *"make things right"* and go directly to the person, there is a veiled intention of:

1. Acquiring an *"I forgive you."*
2. Their apology.
3. A hidden agenda forcing them to acknowledge your humility.
4. To rub it in their face because you're such a *"kind"* and *"forgiving"* person.

The Chair:

I learned a technique many years ago called *"The Chair,"* and it has proven quite effective. I do not know its origin, but it is a timeless and productive method of releasing pent anger, sorrow, unforgiveness, and judgment, especially for ex-spouses.

Sit an empty chair in front of you. Pretend your offender is sitting in it. Express to them everything you can think that they've done to hurt you in any way. Do not waste time excusing or justifying their behavior. After all, they aren't really there. This is exclusively for *you* to release the mess inside of you to replace with holiness. Many times there is screaming and crying—good. Let it all out to leave an empty space ready to usher Holy Spirit in its place.

After you've expressed your heart against them, apologize for holding it against them and forgive them from the heart. Again this is for you, not them. They answer to God for their wrongs. Once you've forgiven them and apologized for your judgment against them, pray and repent to God for the judgment. The only thing left is to simply receive His already granted forgiveness.

If the person or people are deceased, it's much easier because they can no longer offend. If alive, on the other hand, they have ample opportunity to offend again and again. With this, use the *"The Chair"* method each time. Forgiveness is not usually a one-time thing. In my early walk with the Lord, I used it regularly with every offense, big and small. Now it comes naturally and the chair process isn't required. Give no place to the enemy. I decided long ago there is no one on Earth and no offense great enough to let it ruin my intimacy with Christ. When I do struggle with forgiveness or judgment—and I certainly do sometimes, I picture Christ on the cross and remember His words, *"Father, forgive them* [me], *for they [she] know not what they* [she] *do."* If the sinless Son of God can forgive me, who am I to not forgive my ex-husband or anyone else?

Watchman Nee said something that struck a permanent chord in me. It was that our natural man cannot forgive. When we finally recognize and readily admit that in our natural condition, we cannot forgive, we can then say to the Lord, *"I cannot forgive. It is not within my power. However, since I am dead and You are my life, I desire and will allow You to apply Your perfect forgiveness through me."* Brilliant!

Prayer:

Father, in the name of Your Son, Jesus the Christ, thank You for revealing to me how to forgive. I make a choice today to forgive my offender(s). I also repent of my judgment against my ex-spouse with a sincere heart. Remind me constantly that I need the same amount of grace and mercy as they. May I never lose sight of the boundless forgiveness I required and continue to require. Thank You for the gift of Your Son and the loving forgiveness You continuously extend toward me. May You show me how to daily keep my heart pure from the evil of judgment and all unrighteousness. May I never allow any person or Satan to sever my communion with You, my precious Savior and Redeemer. Selah.

Notes

CHAPTER 16

Painful Indiscretions Laid to Rest

Remaining After Offense:

After reading about forgiveness in the previous chapter, it stands to reason that the question on many people's minds is, *"How do I continue to live with them after what they have done against me?"* This is a legitimate question I have asked myself numerous times. As previously mentioned, though my first husband did not physically hit me, the punches he threw were mental, emotional, and sexual.

I ask that you please forgive my openness about sexual abuse because it needs to be noted that sexual abuse goes on within the confines of many marriages, and it is not okay. I state this to clarify for those who may be experiencing this right now. Internally, we know it's wrong, but feel as I once did—because he's my husband, he has the right to do anything he wants.

In my youth, and knowing nothing but the rule *"stay married no matter what,"* it was reasonably simple to forgive him as well as just move on. I begged him to stop his terrible behavior. I told him repeatedly I didn't care what he had done, only that he should start being the husband he was supposed to be. It was altogether painful to remain married to someone who didn't love, like, or respect me; he took every opportunity to belittle me and prey on both friends and strangers to fulfill what should have been my role as his wife. Had he not left me, I honestly don't know if I would have eventually left him, so I cannot speak about what I may have done in later years.

I will also add that just because I "*let it go*," that is not the same as actually moving forward. Since he continuously behaved in such a reckless manner without repentance to God or me, there was no opening to put it behind us; there was only me choosing to ignore the obvious. This chapter is about learning how to genuinely move forward after they have changed their adulterous behavior. Remember, adultery is "*breaking covenant*;" sexual adultery is only one of a myriad of forms.

Although I cannot tell you firsthand how to overcome hurt and pain of the magnitude from my first marriage, I can tell you how I've overcome pain in my current marriage. Even God-ordained marriages are not free of error and obstacles. In my experience, as well as in those who have preceded me, one thing rings loud and clear: when we forgive, everything we do after that must be as unto God. Colossians chapter 3 lays this foundational thinking.

As Unto God:

> Set your mind on the things above, not on the things that are on Earth...But now you also, put them all aside: anger, wrath, malice, slander, and abusive speech from your mouth. Do not lie to one another...as those who have been chosen of God, holy and beloved, put on a heart of compassion, kindness, humility, gentleness and patience; bearing with one another, and forgiving each other, whoever has a complaint against anyone; just as Yahweh forgave you, so also should you. Beyond all these things put on love, which is the perfect bond of unity. Let the peace of Christ rule in your hearts... whatever you do in word or deed, do all in the name of the Lord Jesus, giving thanks through Him to God the Father...

in all things obey those who are your masters on Earth, not with external service, as those who merely please men, but with sincerity of heart, fearing the Lord. Whatever you do, do your work heartily, as for the Lord rather than for men, knowing that from Yahweh you will receive the reward of the inheritance. It is Yahweh Christ whom you serve. For he who does wrong will receive the consequences of the wrong which he has done, and that without partiality (Colossians 3:2, 8-9, 12-15, 17, 22-25).

First, the references are "*slaves*" and "*masters*," we can easily replace them with husband and wife, but do not misunderstand—neither should be slave or master since we are called to "*submit to one another out reverence to Christ* (Ephesians 5:21)." I use this reference to recognize how we are to conduct ourselves specifically within the confines of marriage to actually overcome, not merely have the appearance of overcoming. Way too many marriages look good on the outside because they "*made it work*," but that does not equate overcoming.

I also want to stress the importance of this information and how and when it is best applied. There will be two parts. Section one is for those living with an unrepentant spouse, the second is for moving forward with a spouse who has repented, but you are struggling with faith that they are changed. We must all understand that I am not telling anyone whether or not they should stay or leave, but expressing what to do if you decide that staying is correct according to God. Above all, we are to do everything we do unto God, never unto the person. Never base your actions, good or bad, on "*this will make them love me more*" or "*this will show 'em!*"

Part I: Living with the Unrepentant Spouse:

"Yet if the unbelieving one leaves, let him leave; the brother or the sister is not under bondage in such cases, but God has called us to peace (I Corinthians 7:15)."

Pursue peace with all people, and holiness, without which no one will see Yahweh (Hebrews 7:15, KJV)."

To be honest, there is only so much any human being can endure. God has not called anyone to remain where there is abuse and cheating of various kinds—we are called to peace (Colossians 3:15) and a sound mind (II Timothy 1:7). As mentioned in chapter one, God is more concerned with the individuals within the marriage than the marriage institution. No one is called a slave to men, but free (I Corinthians 7:23).

Some know they are to remain in their marital union for the sake of the ungodly spouse and those who know they must leave (I Corinthians 7:12-16). That being said, the following is for the one who knows they are to remain. Since you stay with a spouse who perpetually sins against you and the marital covenant and you believe God has called you to stay, the only way it will work for the good of God's Kingdom is to learn how to respond to the offender. Staying for the sake of staying is not good—ever. Above in Colossians 3, we read, *"But now you also, put them all aside: anger, wrath, malice, slander, and abusive speech from your mouth. Do not lie to one another...."*

You must ask yourself, *"Can I effectively stay in this marriage and conduct myself in a manner worthy of the gospel of Christ* (Philippians 1:27)?» If not, its time to leave, even if you go only for a season to regroup spiritually, mentally, and emotionally. Sometimes taking a break helps both parties reevaluate the magnitude of the situation.

If you say, *"I'm staying for the Lord,"* yet, everything proceeding from your mouth and attitude is anger, malice, perverse speech, slander, and things of the like, you are not staying for the Lord. Your internal motive is to please someone other than God, albeit church appearance, parents, finances, etc. I am always suspicious of those doing anything *"in the name of Jesus"* when their conduct is most unsavory. Somehow it's justified because their spouse *"deserves"* it. At the end of part II, I will close with how to conduct ourselves in a godly manner in any situation.

Part II: Living with the Repentant Spouse:

If your spouse has broken the covenant vow, but they have confessed and repented, it can be tricky for the offended. In fact, all too often, the repentant one [offender] has a closer walk with Jesus; the offended tends to act so superior that they lose their intimacy with Christ, providing it ever existed as they may have thought.

As I mentioned in my book series, *Discovering the Person of Holy Spirit,* volume 2, chapter 6 entitled, *"Calamity: The Breeding Ground of Faith,"* I openly discuss how Michael had a problem with pornography stemming back to his teen years. Because he was ashamed, it compounded the matter. I will not go into it all since I've already written it in detail, I will skip to my reaction and how God had to change me; a change for which I couldn't be more grateful because God took me to deeper levels of supernatural love.

As the pornography [sexual adultery] was revealed, I calmly threatened him by saying, *"I will not let you destroy this ministry or these children. I will leave you before I let that happen."* Sounds right, doesn't it? To the fleshly man, this is a correct response, but to the Spirit of the Living God whom I serve, my reaction was in every way incorrect. After many months, I traveled to a speaking engagement for the weekend. I found some pornography an hour before leaving. I called Michael on the phone while he was working instead of waiting until I returned. Calm though I was, there was still an underlying threat.

Once at the retreat, Yahweh changed my topic of discussion to *"Love."* It wasn't until I was standing in front of a group of women speaking about love when it hit me: I was not loving Michael as unto Yahweh but unto Michael. Please allow me to elaborate. We love a person intensely, deeply until something goes terribly wrong. This is not the love of God but of man; it is limited, flawed. It is a great love until it becomes tainted by something that displeases us, be it a major or minor issue. Personally, I love him always, but I was expecting him to "*fix his problem*" for my benefit. Of course, I wanted him to fix it with God in mind, but truth be told, it was for me. In my inner man, I thought, "*I, Alexys V. Wolf, minister, author, and founder of The Fiery Sword Ministries, could not be married to such a flawed, ungodly man.*" Hmmm. Can you see the error of my prideful attitude?

Like I said, while speaking before this group, I received a revelation of my error. Upon my return home, my heart had been transformed. I knew he knew a long conversation of chastisement was impending. I had cast shame and guilt, not to mention pressure, upon him leaving him to worry the entire weekend. Somehow, though I knew and taught better, I was conducting myself in a manner suggesting that guilt, pressure, and shame would somehow catapult him into godliness. Tisk, tisk! That never works—not ever—because that is the tactic of God's rival, Satan.

So, I sat beside him and roughly said, "*I love you, not as unto you, but unto God. This issue belongs to you. I will leave it to you to work through in your own time. I will never leave or forsake you. You are my husband, and I am your wife. I apologize for treating you the way I did. I was wrong.*" With this approach, freedom came to him and me!

I had to question my motivation. I had to seek God's face to remind myself of God's true supernatural love and how it should manifest. I had to face the harsh truth that I was subconsciously more concerned about grand-standing and appearance than being obedient to Christ, than extending God's mercy, or lending a helping hand instead of trying to pelt and mutilate him with shame and guilt.

Ladies and gentlemen, I implore you to always check your motives. Just because our conduct is validated by our flesh, that does not make it right in God's sight. In a nutshell, to love as unto God means that we trust God will render reward back to us; that by loving our spouse unconditionally as Christ loves the Church; it is love that will eventually set them free, not our nagging and slandering. Oddly enough, I had taught this many, many times, but in that moment of clarity, I learned on a deeper level how to apply it. Just because we know something doesn›t mean we›re living it.

If we genuinely want a successful marriage, it requires 100% trust and faith that God will accomplish what He says He will, not trust in the person to fulfill all their promises. Mankind can't do all they set out to do. They will disappoint. All we have to do is be obedient to God's love. However, the trust and faith are not in self or our spouse, but in the love of the Almighty. When we love our spouse through their imperfections just as we want to be loved through ours, lives will change—both will be forever transformed. Love, God-love, is not the ushy-gushy mess we emote on Valentine's Day or in the early stages of dating. God is love, but not all forms of love are of God. He is unbiased, impartial, without hypocrisy. God extended mercy and grace to all of mankind, past, present, and future. It's there for you and me. If we believe we need it just as much as one on death row, we'll much more readily extend it to those who have offended us.

If you want to save your marriage with a sincere God-heart instead of mere Law, you must go beyond God-belief into God-trust that His ways are higher; even the demons believe and shutter. You must accept and trust His Word assuring you that pride comes before the fall. It's pride at its most active when you say, *"I am the only one trying to make this marriage work,"* yet belittle the one trying to right their wrongs. Humility will usher Christ's love in the marriage, and it must start with self. You must remember that you need forgiveness for your offenses—hidden and exposed—just as much as your spouse needs forgiveness for theirs. If you trust the Word of God that *"love covers a multitude of sin,"* then you will speak more kindly. When you have something on your heart, be it fear, anger, or whatever, you will approach a discussion with honesty, patience, and kindness.

You must refrain from spewing accusations and slanderous words no matter how much you want to. Remember always that the flesh is at war with God's Spirit within you. The flesh wants to retaliate. The Spirit has already forgiven. Always be honest. Let the ones who have hurt you receive forgiveness. Do not hang it over their head like an apple to a horse, yet always just beyond reach.

In closing, whether you stay or go; whether they confess and repent or don't—do not let personal emotions get the upper hand causing more damage. Don't bury things and pretend they don't exist. Be open and honest, coupled with kindness and love. Never ever use children as leverage against the offender or to get vengeance on your spouse. Children are to be protected, not used as a war weapon. With that, I will end this chapter where it began:

> So, as those who have been chosen of God, holy and beloved, put on a heart of compassion, kindness, humility, gentleness and patience; bearing with one another, and forgiving each other, whoever has a complaint against anyone; just as Yahweh forgave you, so also should you. Beyond all these things put on love, which is the perfect bond of unity. Let the peace of Christ rule in your hearts, to which indeed you were called in one body; and be thankful. Let the word of Christ richly dwell within you, with all wisdom teaching and admonishing one another with psalms and hymns and spiritual songs, singing with thankfulness in your hearts to God. Whatever you do in word or deed, do all in the name of Yahweh Jesus, giving thanks through Him to God the Father (Colossians 3:12-17).

> "For this reason I say to you, her sins, which are many, have been forgiven, for she loved much; but he who is forgiven little, loves little." Then He said to her, "Your sins have been forgiven (Luke 7:47-48)."

Prayer:

Father, help me, oh Lord, to set my mind on things of Heaven and not on the things of this Earth. Move through me, even in the hardest of times, that You may speak and act through me. I thank You, Holy Father, that You have given me everything I need for life; that I will speak as the oracles of God and not as my flesh desires. In the name of Jesus, I command every demon spirit of anger, greed, malice, anxiety, sorrow, depression, chaos, confusion, cowardliness, and every demon of hell to be bound, gagged, and loosed from their assignment over my mind, will and emotions. I declare that I will not be led by anything or anyone other than Holy Spirit. Even in my grief and pain, I choose You, oh Lord, and not my selfish nature of vengeance, for vengeance belongs to You alone. I thank You that You have given me a sound mind, pure heart, and steadfast spirit, and I will walk with You all the days of my life. I will turn neither to the right nor the left, and I will not be double-minded. I stand with, in, and through You. I release everything to You, and I trust You, and You alone. Selah.

Notes

_____

_____

_____

_____

_____

_____

_____

_____

_____

_____

_____

_____

_____

_____

_____

CHAPTER 17

Divorce and all Its Charm

A Three-Strand Cord:

> "And if one can overpower him who is alone, two can resist him. A cord of three strands is not quickly torn apart (Ecclesiastes 4:12)."

In my estimation, the main reason God hates divorce is because He understands to the fullest degree that it is torturous no matter how necessary. Regardless who began the proceedings, how amicable the divorce, no matter how relieved you are to obtain a divorce, it is never easy.

This Scripture above is often used in prayer along with *"Where two or three are gathered together in My name, there I will be in the midst."* You, your prayer partner, and Holy Spirit are a three-strand cord not easily broken. This is power against a strong enemy. Likewise, when you, your spouse, and at least one other witness—plenty more in some cases—come together as one unified in agreement for marriage, it is hard to break. This is why no matter how many miles or years stand between ex-spouses and you, there are lingering effects.

Because I cannot and will not speak for every other divorce in the world, I will speak from personal experience as to how ex-spouses linger though far removed, much like remaining splinters when prying apart those two bonded boards. Early on, we discussed the topic of vows, their importance, and their strong bond. More and more, it becomes glaringly apparent the importance of vows and how unbreakable they are.

Lingering Exes:

At the time of writing this, Michael and I are twenty years into marriage. As you've already read, we are clearly ordained for each other, no question. That being established, I have dreams of both ex-husbands to this day. There are far too many to share details and too many reasons behind them, so I'll focus on a few highlights.

Periodically, I have recurring dreams about both ex-husbands—separately and together. In a dream about one ex-husband, I found myself attracted to him and *"in love"* instead of just *"agape love."* At the end of the dream, I see him running from his wife toward me. He slips two gold wedding rings on my finger. I awoke startled, to say the least! I prayed for God to reveal what I'm to glean from such a dream. I promptly called a friend and prayer partner who also interprets dreams.

Since I know without any doubt I am in love with Michael and have a desire for no other, we were both a bit baffled. Then my friend said, *"Is this to show the depth of how difficult it is to completely sever ties of marriage vows?"* Like a light bulb coming on, I agreed with this interpretation as it registered with my spirit.

We must understand that vows are vows, and God does not take them lightly. Remember the vow Joshua made with the Gibeonites? Though the vow was not made from seeking God, God still expected him to honor it. The Gibeonites were forced into slavery because of their deceit, but also, Joshua was bound to protect them. Translation: Joshua, because he was bound to leave them alive as well as rescue them when they were in trouble, he was, to some extent, bound in slavery to them as they were to him. He was never released from his vow. Even when he was afar, he had to go to them when they called.

To me, that sounds a lot like bondage. Likewise, once we've given ourselves to anyone in marriage, there will always be fragments bound to one another. We cannot deny away an ex-spouse, try though we may. We made memories with them, good or bad. Hearts were broken through marriage and divorce, no matter how minimal or severe. We can't help but wonder, *"How are they? Are they happy or sad? Married or single? Prosperous or bankrupt?"* We can deny they cross our minds and hearts from time to time. It may seem benign, but it is still present, no matter how faint. To this day, dreams of both come and go, much to my chagrin.

The vows we made, albeit foolish, are forever bound to us on some level. This does not mean God did not forgive us or that He does not bless our remarriage. The bottom line is that God hates divorce because it is never a complete departure from the vow [oath] we made before Him and man. It's much like a promise we make to someone. Though we may break our promise and assume it has no lasting effect, the recipient of the broken promise always remembers.

It is of the utmost importance that, before we make a marriage vow or any kind, we are conscious that it is not easily broken. Life and death are in the power of the tongue. Spoken words stick in the spirit realm. They stick in the hearts, minds, souls, and spirits of the recipient. They are not a joke or some random game to play. When we realize not only the value but the power and authority of a vow, we will not so readily make one.

Love vs. In Love:

When I ponder the dreams about my ex-husbands, I realize with great clarity that they are not as far removed from my life as I would have once hoped. We all know that we fall in love with whom we fall in love.

To love is a choice, but with whom we fall in love is not. No matter how we deny true love for another, it doesn't make it less present.

When I married the first time, I loved my husband, but I had been in love with Michael since I was fifteen, yet with no hope of ever marrying him. When I married my second husband, I loved him dearly, but my heart belonged to Michael, not to mention I had made a marital vow to the first husband—double jeopardy; hence the double gold rings in the dream. Try though I may, I could never make myself be in love with either of them the way a wife should eternally love her husband. No matter how hard I tried to not think of Michael or how much I told myself I was not in love with him, it didn't change the fact that I was, irreversibly. When we have to convince ourselves that we are not in love with someone, we can bank on the fact that we are.

Granted, not every person our heart falls for is of God or is the one God created us to marry. Nevertheless, it still doesn't change for whom we long. Never marry someone in hopes of *"getting over"* the other person for whom our heart longs. It is a mistake that will follow us the rest of our lives. The pain will inevitably ensue when we marry someone we love but are not in love. We may put on a good front for a while, years maybe, or even convince ourselves, *"I'm over that other person, and I'm content married to my spouse,"* yet in our hearts, we do not love our spouse as we should.

It is my opinion, and my opinion only, that it is better to stay single and celibate [a eunuch of sorts] than to marry someone we do not love through and through. This act doesn't hurt us alone, but more so, the one we marry. It isn't fair to anyone to give ourselves to someone we cannot give all. With my first marriage, I gave him everything I had based on *"that's just what I'm supposed to do,"* even though he was a nightmare. Michael and I, at that time, were only acquaintances—friends through his family. I had no memories to ponder or long, so it was pretty easy putting him out of my conscious mind and focus on my marriage.

However, Michael and I became best friends after my first husband left me, so I had plenty of memories with my second marriage. Sadly, my mind pondered them far more than I should have or wanted. Although just as with my first marriage, I absolutely gave my second husband everything I had to give, there simply wasn't much to lend, and what I did give was forced from a place desperate to be happy and sane. I was bankrupted from the pain and agony of the first marital disaster, leaving me in the red continually. I tried very hard to be a good wife, to no avail.

Even after being separated by time, space, and several countries for military duties, the thoughts of Michael were ever-present. I denied, and denied, and denied them, ad nauseum, but eventually, I had to admit what was going on in my heart. Of course, I didn't believe in leaving one person to be with another, so I struggled even more. *"How could I do this to such an amazing man as my husband,"* I asked myself repeatedly. Yet I loved who I loved and didn't know what to do. Try though I did, post-divorce, to make it work several times, it just didn't. Unable to bear the thought of being an adulterer, I figured I could date anyone other than Michael because of how it would appear to everyone. I threw myself into the arms of a garden variety of men, but no one replaced my undying love for Michael.

I tried once more to reconcile with my second ex-husband upon the prompting of Holy Spirit. I vowed to God I would give up anything, including my friendship with Michael, my art, and/or modeling. I wanted only God's perfect will for my life. At that point, I had fallen in love with Christ far above Michael, and I was confident that if I was restored to my second ex-husband, God would fill my heart with the love I needed to be a godly, honorable wife. We tried for a time. Since I had committed myself to not being physically intimate with anyone outside marriage, that vow included my ex-husband lest *"ex"* was eliminated. That did not go well with him.

It was looking somewhat positive that we would reunite until he finally said he opted out—my paraphrase. Quite frankly, who could blame him? I certainly could not. He eventually moved on and re-married. Roughly two years later, I married Michael, but not without much prayer and Holy Spirit consent. Once I was sure that God not only approved our union but that it was created by Him, I had peace to move forward. Only with Michael have I ever been whole in a physical marriage. I came to discover that, unless I was with the one I was truly meant to wed, it was far better to be single and celibate than to try to "*replace*" him with someone else. We're right back to the question of "*How does living a lie ever honor God?*"

I know full well the damage I caused many trying to marry someone that did not complete me—pardon the cliché. I cannot stress enough that marriage on Earth is created to be, among other things, a physical depiction of our spiritual marriage to Yeshua, our Great God. Only in Christ do people become whole. In Christ, He completely merges us into Himself. No longer are we two [one God + one person], but we become one in Him. When Michael referred to us as a "*team,*" I told him we are not a team as that suggests more than one person. We are one person, a single unit inseparable.

We are to marry the one God created for us and thus become one unit—better, stronger, more equipped to run the race of Christ. It is not for the purpose of sex, money, status, boredom, loneliness, override sin, or anything of the like. God has a divine purpose for marriage, and it isn't what most people pursue or even realize exists.

Marriage has God-purpose. It is high time people pursue God's purpose instead of thinking of themselves. Before a divorce, ask yourself, "*What God-purpose can come from this?*" Before you marry, ask yourself the exact same question. Before you make any significant decision, ask yourself the same question because it's a good rule of thumb, period. Problems will begin to minimize.

Notes

CHAPTER 18

What about the Children?

"Do not be deceived, God is not mocked; for whatever a man sows, this he will also reap. For the one who sows to his own flesh will from the flesh reap corruption, but the one who sows to the Spirit will from the Spirit reap eternal life (Galatians 6:7-8)."

But it shall come about, if you do not obey the Lord your God, to observe to do all His commandments and His statutes with which I charge you today, that all these curses will come upon you and overtake you…your sons and your daughters shall be given to another people, while your eyes look on and yearn for them continually; but there will be nothing you can do. A people whom you do not know shall eat up the produce of your ground and all your labors, and you will never be anything but oppressed and crushed continually (Deuteronomy 28:15, 32-33).

Can't Change the Facts:

Without a doubt, this chapter is for everyone. If you have already made significant relational blunders, there is always a way to correct—not undo—things through Christ. However, this is especially for those who have yet to make life-altering decisions regarding marriage and divorce. The fact that there are repercussions to every action is common knowledge. It's as simple as 2+2=4. No one can change the math, no matter how they try. The sentence above, "*Your sons and your daughters shall be given to another people*," should be startling to everyone, hence we should count the cost before we make life-altering decisions not in alignment with Christ.

So it is with the decisions we make today. The invisible seed—spiritual and intangible—we plant will produce according to the seed, not according to what we want it to grow. No matter how much we would like 2+2 to equal 3 or 5 or any other number, it will always equal 4, bar none. If you plant corn and later want beans, you still have corn more abundantly.

Notice that these verses above do not specifically apply to the Christ-follower but to all of mankind. God's Law affects the Earth whether one chooses to follow Christ or not. The law of increase, for instance, set in motion in the Garden of Eden, was created for increased blessings. Remember, after the fall of man, the law of increase remained, but it worked against mankind instead of for man. So it is today. No matter the person, Christian or non-Christian, disobedience to God's will will cause curses [chaos, confusion, discord, trials, tribulations] to come upon you and those around you. This is why it is of the utmost importance to understand obedience according to God, not just your local church.

Enemies of the Cross:

If we, God's people, refuse to look at what true obedience is in the sight of God, we will continue down a crooked path of future destruction, all the while calling it "*of God*" because it seems good on the surface. We live in a day of absolute godlessness—a "*pre-Christ*" period. Philippians 3:18-19 reads, "*For many walk, of whom I have told you often, and now tell you even weeping, that they are the enemies of the cross of Christ: Whose end is destruction, whose god is their belly, and whose glory is in their shame, who mind earthly things* (KJV).»

Notice that it reads, «*Enemies of the cross*" and "*whose glory is their shame.*" These are vital elements determining our future, specifically in romantic relationships, whether they lead to marriage and/ or divorce. When we engage in premarital sexual activity or marry someone with whom we are not ordained because we did not seek God's holiness and perfect will in either situation, future problems are being planted by seed we refuse to acknowledge. We just let the proverbial chips [spiritual seed] fall where they may with no regard how it will affect and harm others [self, family, or future children] later in life.

It is of the utmost importance that we seek the Kingdom of God and His righteousness now so that later we will have peace and rest instead of having to constantly beg God to release us from the mess we made by our own «*appetite.*" The things we do driven by our fleshly man are shameful, yet, as Paul writes in Philippians, become our glory, or rather, our point of pride and delight. I often see where people who succumb to lust end in bad marriages, worse divorces, and several children lost and torn apart by their parents. Children suffer the most at the hand of our foolish, godless decisions and are used as bait to get revenge on the one they couldn't wait to bed, yet now hate to the uttermost.

Glory in Their Shame:

Here is an all too common hypothetical. Two people from anywhere meet. They're very attracted to one another, assuming their lust is love and engage in sexual intercourse too soon. At first, their "*glory is their shame,*" meaning they may joke lightly or brag about their indiscretions—that which is shameful but perceived as something in which to revel. They justify their ungodly conduct by the measure of how much they "*love each other*" and "*God will forgive us.*" As I have written in previous books, "*forgiveness*" or "*being separated from God's love"* is never the issue. Christ extended forgiveness to everyone at the cross because of His unfailing love. The problem is blocking the blessings Yahweh longs to bestow His people.

The couple eventually marries. They have children. Sometime in the future, they decide to divorce, whether it was caused by adultery, boredom, career, or any other excuse. Love is replaced by hatred. The children love both parents. The parents say, "*I love my children,*" yet around every bend of their twisted road, they use their kids as pawns to gouge a knife into their ex-spouse's back.

The mother will teach her kids unhealthy things, and the father will turn and discipline the kids for the mothers poor decision as though the child did something wrong. The father will badmouth their mother just to make himself feel better. I have seen where both parents, at some point, had an affair, yet both assault the other for it, all the while justifying their own misgivings. Both will fill their childrens heads with hateful words against the other and justify it with, «*I'm just telling them the truth,*" but all they are really doing is exerting a feeble attempt to hurt their ex-spouse. Maybe one parent had an affair, so the one who didn't constantly insults the one who did in front of the children. Simultaneously, the one who did not cheat is now engaging in sexual activity, refusing to acknowledge that their behavior is just as ungodly and destructive as the one who had an affair.

Hurting the Children:

There are countless scenarios where parents hurt the children because they are so exceedingly frustrated with themselves, their ex-spouse or soon-to-be-ex, and their life as a whole. Things did not turn out as they had hoped, and the kids ended up bearing the brunt of their anxieties. Rarely do the parents take a hard look into the spiritual mirror to assess their culpability leading to the bitter, broken road they find themselves. It's as though it would be irreversibly painful to look at themselves, to take accountability for their own personal actions. Yet, things will only worsen for everyone involved, most definitely the children, until they do.

Many onlookers wonder how the parents can be so cruel and blind. Furthermore and more importantly, everyone seems to be asking, «*How could God let this happen? These children don't deserve such abuse.*" The answer to this is written all throughout God's Word. He gave us guidelines for this earthly walk. He gave us explicit instruction and, with that instruction, openly revealed the repercussions of both holy and unholy behavior. He has not left mankind abandoned, yet, because of our blatant disobedience, folly falls upon our heads, and we don't have enough insight to recognize it.

If—and this is a big "*if*"—those who claim to be Christ-followers would stop playing church and become the Church as God designed us to be, we would much more quickly fall in love with the One True God. We would follow His instruction from our love for YHWH instead of religious rhetoric and save ourselves from the destruction resulting from disobedience. This shift would stop us from thinking everything bad is God's perpetual punishment or that God has abandoned His people. When we shift into Kingdom thinking, we will become better parents equipped to build our children instead of destroying them.

Notice in Deuteronomy 28:32-33 above—I recommend reading the entire chapter—states what will happen as a result of disobedience: "*Your sons and your daughters shall be given to another people, while your eyes look on and yearn for them continually; but there will be nothing you can do. A people whom you do not know shall eat up the produce of your ground and all your labors, and you will never be anything but oppressed and crushed continually.*"

How much do we see today? Because of fornication, sexual adultery, and unholy matrimony, children are being raised by "*another people*"—stepfathers and mothers, foster parents, grandparents, total strangers, abusers, pedophiles, etc.—and there is "*nothing you can do.*" It is a tragedy of astronomical proportion, but no one blames us.

Oh, that we would awaken to truth, abide His Word, seek the wisdom of His instruction, understand He gave us authority over our lives, and that we, generally speaking, do to ourselves what comes upon us.

"Oppressed and crushed continually" is exactly what is happening because of our negligence to His Word. Unless we come to a place of absolute submission to our Lord and Savior, continued curses will befall us. This is the Word. It is as plain as day, yet we continue to misuse the authority God has given and turn and blame Him. So many people rationalize that *"there are no more curses because He bore the curse."* Yes, absolutely, He bore our curse, but we must take His cross so that the blood He shed will be appropriately applied to everyday life. Otherwise, the curses remain and continue to mound though we can't seem to figure out why. Disobedience is the *"why."* Repentance through humility is the solution. Too many want to cry out to God to *"fix things"* absent of repentance, absent of admission to their own error, or a desire and action toward transformation.

Our Appetites are Our God:

How much longer will our appetites be our god? How much longer will we refuse to acknowledge His instruction? How much longer will we reject His heart of love toward mankind simply because we do not want to die to ourselves, our fleshly nature? How much longer will we bind the hand of blessings because we constantly release the flesh's desires? Ladies and gentlemen, we reap whatever we sow, be it corn into the Earth's ground or whether we sow obedience or disobedience into the spiritual realm. This cannot be undone. Furthermore, whatever we sow, we will reap an increased harvest since the harvest is always much larger than the tiny seed planted.

If we really want to see our lives change in our country or the Earth, we must first submit to our most holy God in absolute humility. Want to see your children stop crying? Submit your whole heart. Want to see depression dissipate? Submit. Want to see the divorce rate drop, disease diminish, rebellious children relent, for holiness to come into an unholy land? It begins with one—you. It's time to stop playing around with God, with His Word, with His heart. When we stop pretending to be such good Christ-followers doing *"the church thing,"* we will stop entering into unholy covenant, sexual relationships outside marriage, situations where divorced parents use their children as a ball in a tennis match, and many things of the like. How many countless people I counsel proclaim to love Yahweh but refuse to stop having sex outside marriage. These same people then come to me in a panic because they—the couple or just the female who has been abandoned—have gotten pregnant and don't know what they're going to do.

How many women get angry because a man dumped them when they became pregnant, and the woman acts like it's all the man's fault? How many women have justified abortion because the man was ungodly and didn't want to have a baby with such a *"terrible person?"* If all of these people having premarital sex would stop listening to their minds, wills, emotions, and hearts and wait upon Yahweh's perfect timing, the world would be much more peaceful. There would be far fewer children from broken homes and unwed parents.

Women would stop agonizing over the decision to kill their unborn children. Men would learn to commit to God and the woman God designed for them becoming the Kingdom-minded person God called him to be. There would be fewer children in the government's system because they would not exist or they would be in safe homes. The changes are endless, yet few are willing to think beyond their emotions and sexual urges to make such changes.

It's time to see God's perfect plan and willingly wait for it to come to fruition. Marriage is sacred to God. People are sacred to God. It is we who disregard His perfect design. Think of how many children would be raised whole, holy, without rejection, without fear, without being torn apart, if the next generation would seek God's face before taking action. People have caused the world's mess the church is in, kids are in, and we are in. We must choose to take responsibility, not only responsibility but action toward what the Lord has ordained. When we become Kingdom-minded, we will see everything so much clearer regarding the sanctity of marriage, sex, and all things holy. Think before you leap. Pray before you act. Prepare yourself for the future to have an excellent harvest to reap. Let Deuteronomy 28:1-14 be your guide. It reads as follows:

> "Now it shall be, if you diligently obey Yahweh your God, being careful to do all His commandments which I command you today, Yahweh your God will set you high above all the nations of the Earth. All these blessings will come upon you and overtake you if you obey Yahweh your God:
>
> ³ Blessed shall you be in the city, and blessed shall you be in the country.
>
> ⁴ Blessed shall be the offspring of your body and the produce of your ground and the offspring of your beasts, the increase of your herd and the young of your flock.
>
> ⁵ Blessed shall be your basket and your kneading bowl.
>
> ⁶ Blessed shall you be when you come in, and blessed shall you be when you go out.
>
> ⁷ Yahweh shall cause your enemies who rise up against you to be defeated before you; they will come out against you one way and will flee before you seven ways.
>
> ⁸ Yahweh will command the blessing upon you in your barns and in all that you put your hand to, and He will bless you in the land which Yahweh your God gives you.
>
> ⁹ Yahweh will establish you as a holy people to Himself, as He swore to you, if you keep the commandments of Yahweh your God and walk in His ways.

¹⁰ So all the peoples of the Earth will see that you are called by the name of Yahweh, and they will be afraid of you.

¹¹ Yahweh will make you abound in prosperity, in the offspring of your body and in the offspring of your beast and in the produce of your ground, in the land which Yahweh swore to your fathers to give you.

¹² Yahweh will open for you His good storehouse, the Heavens, to give rain to your land in its season and to bless all the work of your hand; and you shall lend to many nations, but you shall not borrow.

¹³ Yahweh will make you the head and not the tail, and you only will be above, and you will not be underneath, if you listen to the commandments of Yahweh your God, which I charge you today, to observe them carefully,

¹⁴ and do not turn aside from any of the words which I command you today, to the right or to the left, to go after other gods to serve them."

Prayer:

Yahweh, I cry out to You for mercy! I desire to right my wrongs where my children are concerned. Show me how to lead my children into righteousness, healing, wholeness, purity, forgiveness, and anything of You. Forgive my selfish indiscretions that dishonor You and that dishonor my children. Whatever emotions I may have about marriage or divorce guide me to where the feelings no longer run my life. I repent in total humility of making myself an idol before You. Thank You for Your forgiveness and mercy. Help me to finish reaping this bad field that I've sown that I may one day reap the harvest of my new good seed I'm planting in my family and in my life. Amen.

Notes

CHAPTER 19

Overcoming the Lie

"There is therefore now no condemnation to them which are in Christ Jesus, who walk not after the flesh, but after the Spirit (Romans 8:1, KJV)."

Condemnation, Shame, Fear and Guilt:

Definition of Condemnation: 1. To express strong disapproval of; 2. To pronounce judicial sentence on; 3. To demonstrate the guilt of; 4. To judge or pronounce unfit for use.

Definition of Shame: 1. a painful emotion caused by a strong sense of *guilt*, embarrassment; 2. one that brings dishonor, disgrace, or condemnation; 3. a great disappointment

Definition of Fear: 1. a distressing emotion aroused by impending danger, evil, pain, etc. real or imagined; 2. a specific instance of or propensity for such a feeling; phobia; 3. concern or anxiety; solicitude; 4. reverential awe, especially toward God; the fear of God; 5. something that causes feelings of dread or apprehension

Definition of Guilt: 1. the fact of having committed a breach of conduct especially violating law and involving a penalty; 2. feelings of culpability especially for imagined offenses or from a sense of inadequacy

Definition of Conviction: 1. The act or process of convincing; 2. The state of being convinced

To understand how to overcome the lie of guilt, shame, condemnation, and fear in any given situation, we must first understand that these things are never from God—never. Alas, the majority of Christ's body doesn't seem to know the difference between those things and conviction. They are vastly different. Guilt, shame, fear, and condemnation can be grouped as one, and they all come from the enemy seeking to kill, steal, and destroy the Kingdom of God and us within it. Conviction comes from God.

For the one not walking according to the flesh, but according to Holy Spirit, condemnation is null and void. Guilt and shame should have zero placement after one has repented of sin and walking according to Holy Spirit. Forgiveness was complete at the cross. Once Christ was buried, the sinful nature of all mankind was buried with Him. New life and the new, spotless bloodline became available to all at the resurrection. If we have received the new blood by repenting of that which offended God, condemnation is always from Satan. Once we realize it is of the enemy, we can much more readily pull it down, out, and away from us.

We can never undo a wrong. We can, of course, make it right, but we cannot take back an improper action. Only God can rectify that which we have defiled. We can also stand in the promise mentioned in many of the previous chapters of *«that which Satan meant against us for evil, God can and will turn around for good if we love Him* (Romans 8:28).» And that is not just our good, but the good of God's Kingdom.

In the garden, Adam and Eve walked naked. This was not shameful because they were as God created them, pure and sinless. However, once they disobeyed God's command, suddenly, they covered themselves and hid. Why did they hide? Shame. Fear. Guilt. Condemnation. Since sin is of Satan, so are the repercussions. Satan wants the original form [upright, guiltless, shameless, pure, and holy] of that which was created in God's image [mankind] to take his image [guilty, shameful, impure, unholy, crooked and flat on our faces cowering in a fetal position].

These four feelings come in a vast array of forms. Satan will prey upon us through them easily and readily because it is of him, not God. These are all tools of the enemy to keep us oppressed and downtrodden. He utilizes them to the fullest degree to keep us from our God-destiny, from our divine healing, freedom, peace, and all things God. Some levels of shame, fear, guilt, and condemnation are fairly easy to overcome. Other levels, however, take a lifetime of *"pulling down"* and overcoming, such as divorce, murder, or any treacherous act done outside of God's will.

We have all done things we are not pleased to have exposed. There are no exemptions, but this is why Christ died. For God's people to act as though Christ's blood is insufficient is to blaspheme Jesus Christ—His death, burial, and resurrection. He came, not for the righteous, but the unrighteous. He came, not for the unblemished, but the severely blemished; not the moral, but the immoral. As my friend, Pastor Mike Turner, says, *"Christ came, not to make the immoral moral, but to give life to the dead."*

You and I, people past, present, and future, are condemned to death outside of Christ. Our flesh is cursed. Everyone has shame, guilt, and/or condemnation from something, lest they one, have no conscience or two, they've learned how to overcome it by the blood of the Lamb. Even if we are the latter, there are times when we must overcome because some strongholds just do not want to release. *"And they overcame him by the blood of the Lamb, and by the word of their testimony, and they loved not their lives unto the death,*" states Revelation 12:11 (KJV).

The "How-To" of Overcoming:

Here's the "*how-to*" part. I can think of only one thing in my life where those satanic strongholds re-emerge more often than any other, and that is leaving my second husband. He was such a good guy, and he loved me. Regardless of his flaws, he didn't deserve my rejection or the emotional roller coaster ride through which I took him. Although I did not intend to be hurtful, given my disastrous emotional and mental condition, I hurt him all the same. Even though he is happily remarried and thriving, there are moments when I run into someone who "*knew us when,*" that shame and guilt are ever-present, seeking an opportunity to pounce upon my head and heart.

When that happens, instead of falling into a heap in the fetal position, I quickly remind myself of who I am in Christ by His blood. I put into use II Corinthians 10:3-6, which reads, «*For though we walk in the flesh, we do not war according to the flesh, for the weapons of our warfare are not of the flesh, but divinely powerful for the destruction of fortresses. We are destroying speculations and every lofty thing raised up against the knowledge of God, and we are taking every thought captive to the obedience of Christ. We are ready to punish all disobedience whenever your obedience is complete.*"

I, on purpose, take authority over my mind, heart, and body pulling down everything not planted in me by God. Shame, fear, condemnation, and guilt are lies from the enemy—always. If we have repented and received forgiveness for whatever sin we committed in the past, pull down those lingering side effects. Or, in other words, pull out the lie that says, "*You are not forgiven*" or "*You will never be of any God-use again*" or "*God could never love someone as useless and vile as you. You will never be any good to anyone, especially God. Look what you did.*"

Ladies and gentlemen, Christ died for you just as much as for everyone. He died for your sinful nature, not just the individual sins.

You weren't born when He died for you. Take the authority vested in you by Christ and get rid of all of the guilt, fear, condemnation, and shame. Otherwise, you are basically saying that Christ's sacrifice is insufficient. Later, we will cover more extensively II Corinthians 5. Paul refers to the human body as a "*tent*," causing us to groan and be burdened. Satan is vastly aware of how the "*tent*" is opposed to the Spirit of the Living God, and he uses it against us any way he can.

It is imperative to understand that God moves us Spirit-to-spirit in our inner being, but Satan moves us from our flesh, our outer man. Flesh is all he has to use to manipulate the born-again believer and, without a doubt, he uses it to the utmost. If he can't get to us with our wallet, sex, greed, or things of the like, he'll get us in our minds. The mind is talked about all throughout the Bible. The mind is where sin is conceived before it is birthed. If he can convince us of our uselessness before Almighty God, he has us in his clutch! Below are just a few of many texts on the mind to help us remember that guilt, shame, fear, and condemnation are a matter of the mind and heart, the place within us that controls everything we do.

Staying Your Focus on Things Above:

"And do not be conformed to this world, but be transformed by the renewing of your mind, so that you may prove what God's will is, that which is good and acceptable and perfect (Romans 12:2)."

Rejoice in Yahweh always; again I will say, rejoice! Let your gentle spirit be known to all men. Yahweh is near. Be anxious for nothing, but in everything by prayer and supplication with thanksgiving let your requests be made known to God. And the peace of God, which surpasses all comprehension, will guard your hearts and your minds in Christ Jesus. Finally, brethren, whatever is true, whatever is honorable, whatever is right, whatever is pure, whatever is lovely, whatever is of good repute, if there is any excellence and if anything worthy of praise, dwell on these things. The things you have learned and received and heard and seen in me, practice these things, and the God of peace will be with you (Philippians 4:4-9).

"For God hath not given us the spirit of fear; but of power, and of love, and of a sound mind (2 Timothy 1:7, KJV)."

"The steadfast of mind You will keep in perfect peace, because he trusts in You (Isaiah 26:3)."

"Watch over your heart with all diligence, for from it flow the springs of life (Proverbs 4:23)."

"But I see a different law in the members of my body, waging war against the law of my mind and making me a prisoner of the law of sin which is in my members (Romans 7:23)."

But if any of you lacks wisdom, let him ask of God, who gives to all generously and without reproach, and it will be given to him. But he must ask in faith without any doubting, for the one who doubts is like the surf of the sea, driven and tossed by the wind. For that man ought not to expect that he will receive anything from Yahweh, being a double-minded man, unstable in all his ways (James 1:5-8).

"Let this mind be in you, which was also in Christ Jesus (Philippians 2:5, KJV)."

"But I say to you that everyone who looks at a woman with lust for her has already committed adultery with her in his heart: (Matthew 5:28)."

In the above Scriptures, notice the words *"peace, sound mind, law of my mind, law of sin, heart, rejoice, thanksgiving, double-minded, waging war."* I cannot stress enough that guilt, fear, shame, and condemnation are a lie of the enemy. They wage war against our minds and hearts. If we allow them to overtake us—and it is a choice—Satan has won.

We live in a society where we, Christ-followers, give more validity to Satan than to God. We empower Satan and dethrone Christ daily and don't even realize. We do it by allowing Satan's deceptive ways to mandate our conduct instead of Holy Spirit who lives within. It is a tragedy of astronomical proportion, and it must cease. More specifically, it happens with those who have been divorced. It happens to those who have not yet married because we are led, not by Holy Spirit, but emotions. It happens to those who choose celibacy, but because of double-mindedness, cave thinking to themselves, *"What's the use? I'm already condemned from my past actions."*

We must, we must, we must comprehend in our innermost being that when Christ died for our sin nature, He didn't remain dead! He overcame death and the grave! In this, He overcame our sinful past, present, and future. It's high time we begin living mindful of this. Stop allowing the enemy's lies [guilt, fear, shame, condemnation] to control who you are and will become. Take control over your every thought, pull down what is not of God, condemn it to death in the name of Jesus Christ, and re-align with He who conquered everything of Satan on our behalf.

Prayer:

Father, because of the bloodshed on Calvary for me, I release every ounce of shame, lies, fear, guilt, and condemnation over to You. Father, remind me of who I am in You. Jesus, You gave Your life that I could walk as a free person on this Earth. May I never forsake or reject what You have given as a gift to me. May I walk upright in heart and spirit, knowing that I have been redeemed from my sins, past, present, and future. I thank You that I no longer have to carry the load of guilt and reproach I brought upon myself. I release it all to You and receive the new robe of righteousness set aside by You just for me! Blessings to You, great God of Heaven and Earth! Amen!

Notes

CHAPTER 20

Becoming Whole

For we who are in this tent groan, being burdened, not because we want to be unclothed, but further clothed, that mortality may be swallowed up by life. Now He who has prepared us for this very thing is God, who also has given us the Spirit as a guarantee. So we are always confident, knowing that while we are at home in the body we are absent from Yahweh. For we walk by faith, not by sight. We are confident, yes, well pleased rather to be absent from the body and to be present with Yahweh. Therefore we make it our aim, whether present or absent, to be well pleasing to Him. For we must all appear before the judgment seat of Christ, that each one may receive the things done in the body, according to what he has done, whether good or bad. Knowing, therefore, the terror of Yahweh, we persuade men; but we are well known to God, and I also trust are well known in your consciences...for the love of Christ compels us...therefore, if anyone is in Christ, he is a new creation; old things have passed away; behold, all things have become new. Now all things are of God, who has reconciled us to Himself through Jesus Christ, and has given us the ministry of reconciliation, that is, that God was in Christ reconciling the world to Himself, not imputing their trespasses to them, and has committed to us the word of reconciliation. Now then, we are ambassadors for Christ, as though God were pleading through us: we implore you on Christ's behalf, be reconciled to God. For He made Him who knew no sin to be sin for us, that we might become the righteousness of God in Him (II Corinthians 5:4-11, 14, 17-21, NKJV).

Fear of God is the Base, Love is the Offspring:

We have all struggled with wholeness wondering if it's attainable and how it should look or feel. We struggle with our past, with our present, and with our future. We toil dealing with past mistakes, hoping in the present not to make future mistakes, and with the future, wondering if our past will always taint it. It is madness outside Christ's mind. II Corinthians 5 attests to this. Paul refers to this mortal body as a *"tent."* We groan and are burdened by it. He mentions being well pleased to be freed of this body and present with YHWH—for that is true and utter wholeness.

Paul continues that we will all be judged for our every action—good and bad, but just before that information, he reassures us that God has prepared us for this journey by leaving us the Guarantee [Holy Spirit]. Paul makes it known that they know the terror of Yahweh, so they are compelled by the love of Christ. On the surface, one might consider this a grave contradiction. We are told repeatedly that the *"fear of Yahweh is the beginning of wisdom"* in both the Old and New Testaments. However, I John 4:18 reads, *"There is no fear in love; but perfect love casts out fear, because fear involves punishment, and the one who fears is not perfected in love."*

It is of the utmost importance to fear Yahweh, but as we develop our intimate relationship with Him, love will always override the fear. If fear involves punishment, we should only walk in fear of God when disobedient to His will. Once we step into the realm of complete obedience, our heart is 100% consigned to His will—love is our compulsion far exceeding fear. Though fear is the base, love is the offspring [the growth of good fruit]. His boundless love is the fruit we bear in His name. His love is wholeness. His love is what motivates us to do anything, the drive that moves us to action.

It is His limitless love allowing us to walk in faith. Faith will enable us to accept His renewal while still in this tent causing such groaning. Once we have reconciled ourselves unto God completely, we fully possess His wholeness; we merge with Him in the oneness discussed throughout these pages. Therefore, all that is in Christ is making us a new creation. We pass from death unto life while still residing in a defiled tent. Yahweh's most earnest desire is to transition us into His life to honor the King and expand His Kingdom while living on Earth. Every decision we make after that is God-focused, God-honoring, God-driven.

The Kingdom, Our Driving Force

Whether we are single for the first time, married, single again from divorce or widowed, or considering marriage or divorce, Christ and His Kingdom within us are to be our sole driving force, never our fleshly desires. We need then to avoid making mistakes of old— ours or someone else's. We no longer want to go into any vow or agreement without first consulting Yeshuah, just as in days of old when God's people sought His face first before making a move. In I Corinthians 10:1-14, 21-24, 31), let's investigate the following text. I've blocked it into sections.

> a. For I do not want you to be unaware, brethren, that our fathers were all under the cloud and all passed through the sea, and all were baptized into Moses in the cloud and in the sea, and all ate the same spiritual food; and all drank the same spiritual drink, for they were drinking from a spiritual rock which followed them, and the rock was Christ (vs. 1-4).

In section (a) we see that in the time of Moses leading God's people out of Egypt, they all were under the same direction—Jesus Christ, The Rock. Today, within the body of Christ, we all have the same Rock to follow and to follow us. This is simply a statement reminding us that we all have the same Lord, no matter pre or post-Calvary, no matter what our situation or circumstance.

> b. Nevertheless, with most of them God was not well-pleased; for they were laid low in the wilderness (vs 5). Now these things happened as examples for us, so that we would not crave evil things as they also craved.

In section (b), we plainly see that God was displeased with the vast majority. Our predecessors of Christ are an example for all of us. We simply choose whether or not to make the same mistakes as they or follow Christ's path in obedience receiving His bountiful, eternal blessings. His most earnest desire for us, because of His everlasting love, is that we heed the warning and not fall prey to the cravings of evil, our fleshly man.

> c. Now these things happened as examples for us, so that we would not crave evil things as they also craved. Do not be idolaters, as some of them were; as it is written, "The people sat down to eat and drink, and stood up to play (vs. 6-7).

Section (c) needs special notation because it's quickly glossed over when reading. We are called to shun idolatry. This is vital to our wholeness since our wholeness comes implicitly from God. We can receive wholeness from God only when our hearts are entirely consigned to Christ. There is no room for us to grant access to anything that would usurp God's place "*as*" [He completely overtakes us] not "*in*" [He has merely a tiny section] our hearts. Idolatry fractures. Idolatry shatters us in a million pieces because it leads away from

God. Idolatry is Satan's bait. Placing self-will above God's will is idolatry. Let us heed the failures of those who have gone before us so as not to make the same mistakes. History need not repeat itself.

> d. Nor let us act immorally, as some of them did, and twenty-three thousand fell in one day (vs. 8).

Section (d) references immorality specifically. God does not leave us without instruction, though so many times, we act as if He has. Corruption begins in the mind. When our minds are flooded with immoral thoughts, it leads away from God. Again, God is our only hope for wholeness. Even when it appears harmless, we eventually manifest immoral conduct when we drift. In this, guilt and shame overtake us, and we remain shattered. We justify immorality with the "but-thoughts:" *"But I love him or her so it's okay if we have sex"* or *"But God knows how lonely and hurt I am"* or *"But I need to do this or that to feel better."* Any *"but-thoughts"* of the like are immoral and idolatrous at the root—they are self-focused and self-motivated. When our focus is on ourselves, it is rooted in pride. Anything rooted in pride will lead, without a doubt, to destruction. Wholeness, then, will elude us and become seemingly unattainable.

> e. Nor let us try the Lord, as some of them did, and were **destroyed** by the serpents (vs. 9).

Section (e) addresses the trying of Yahweh as they did in the wilderness. The end result is death by serpents. Whether these serpents are literal or spiritual [demonic forces] is irrelevant. The fact remains that they clearly neither feared nor loved the Lord. If you seek wholeness, you must turn away from any form of disobedience.

> f. Nor grumble, as some of them did, and were **destroyed** by the destroyer (vs. 10).

Section (f) is one of my favorites because it keeps me on point in my walk of wholeness. It's worth reading, re-reading, and meditating, *"Nor grumble, as some of them did, and were destroyed by the destroyer."* This could encompass an entire book! My third book, *Looking for God volume 2*, expounds upon this topic in chapters 18 and 19, *"Kingdom Objective"* and *"Rejoice!"* They are dedicated to murmuring and complaining because mankind is prone to it. If we do not understand we are to praise Him in the good times and more so in the bad, wholeness will be unattainable. Praise ushers Holy Spirit and confounds the enemy. Holy Spirit is the great Comforter. When we complain, we exert our inner lack of faith, an issue with everyone. When we choose to complain in any situation, we open the door widely to Satan. When given enough latitude, Satan will destroy God's people—you.

> g. Now these things happened to them as an example, and they were written for our instruction, upon whom the ends of the ages have come. Therefore let him who thinks he stands take heed that he does not fall (vs. 11-12).

Section (g) merely reiterates how these things happened as an example for us. Again, pride is addressed. If you think you stand, take warning. This is the word to God's people, not the lost. Pride is running rampant among the body of Christ, and it will kill the vast majority. Only a remnant will remain in the end. Check your personal pride level. The more willingly we expunge it from your tent, the faster wholeness will overtake us.

> h. No temptation has overtaken you but such as is common to man; and God is faithful, who will not allow you to be tempted beyond what you are able, but with the temptation will provide the way of escape also, so that you will be able to endure it (vs. 13).

Section (h) is one of the most commonly misquoted verses in the entire Bible. Many misquote, *"God won't give me more burdens than I can handle."* Instead, the Word states that God will not allow us to be tempted beyond what is common to man or more than one can overcome. He always gives way out, always equips us to endure, and, most importantly, He is always faithful. The way out is choosing to be led by Holy Spirit instead of fleshly emotion or desire. The ability to endure is focusing on the Kingdom of God instead of anything else. In a nutshell, our wholeness does not come from being *"strong enough"* to endure but being *"weak enough"* to rely on the Great Comforter instead of anything of self.

> i. Therefore, my beloved, flee from idolatry...you cannot drink the cup of YHWH and the cup of demons; you cannot partake of the table of YHWH and the table of demons. Or do we provoke YHWH to jealousy? We are not stronger than He, are we? All things are lawful, but not all things are profitable. All things are lawful, but not all things edify (vs. 14, 21-23).

Section (i) is quite simple—choose life or death, Christ or Satan, the Spirit or the flesh. Attempting to select both on any level is choosing insanity—being shattered and scattered. Just because we have *"the right"* to choose something does not make it suitable for us or for anyone else. Plainly and simply stated, flee idolatry. We're back to the same as section (c). Idolatry is always a vine from the seed and root of pride. Pride will destroy us and remove every ounce of wholeness ever attained or sought.

> j. Let no one seek his own good, but that of his neighbor... whether, then, you eat or drink or whatever you do, do all to the glory of God (vs. 24, 31).

Section (j) gives a summation, which is to do all for Christ's glory. Never are we to decide based on the soul [mind, will, and emotion]. When we do, we fail.

To bring all this into the topic of marriage and divorce, we must see the bigger picture. Too often, we marry and divorce for all of the wrong reasons. We enter an unholy covenant because we did not seek the Father's instruction. Therefore we were unable to see the destructive end result. Whether we stay or go in a non-God-ordained marriage, it is a condition of being shattered inwardly. We exit unions based on the wrong reasons and compound our shattered condition.

There is hope for wholeness, no matter where we are, our situation, or what we contemplate or have already executed. We must understand that wholeness does not come from anything changing other than self and our level of intimacy with God. No matter what, wholeness is ushered exclusively by the Holy Spirit through our obedience toward Him.

Keys to Wholeness:

> Then God appeared to Solomon at night and said to him, "I have heard your prayer and have chosen this place for Myself as a house of sacrifice. If I shut up the heavens so that there is no rain, or if I command the locust to devour the land, or if I send pestilence among My people, and My people who are called by My name humble themselves and pray and seek My face and turn from their wicked ways, then I will hear from Heaven, will forgive their sin and will heal their land. Now My eyes will be open and My ears attentive to the prayer offered in this place. For now I have chosen and consecrated this house that My name may be there forever, and My eyes and My heart will be there perpetually. As for you, if you walk before Me as your father David walked, even to do

according to all that I have commanded you, and will keep My statutes and My ordinances, then I will establish your royal throne as I covenanted with your father David, saying, "You shall not lack a man to be ruler in Israel (II Chronicle 7:12-18)."

God's people were in bad shape because of their disobedience and foolish decisions. I want to point to several key elements leading to wholeness:

1. God heard—know that He hears when you cry out to Him
2. My people—know that you are God's people
3. Humble yourself
4. Pray
5. Seek God's will
6. Turn from sin
7. Hear God's voice
8. Forgive because you are fogiven
9. Open your heart, spirit, soul, and mind to God
10. Chosen—know you are a chosen people
11. Consecrated [sacred to God]
12. My name—it's all about God and His Holy Name, not your name
13. Royal—you are royal in Christ
14. Established—He will establish your royal throne [a place in His royal Kingdom]

Following these simple and specific instructions will usher wholeness. Solomon cried out to God in humble prayer, and Yahweh heard. Then he instructed him as to what needed to be done for restoration. Humility was vital for God to hear and attend. Seeking God's face instead of seeking to *"do good deeds"* is crucial. Religious acts will never make one whole. Trying to be *"like Christ"* is not the same as allowing Christ full access to rule in our hearts and be Himself through us. Letting God "*live in you*" is not the same as Christ "*becoming your life.*" Small words make a huge difference.

Prayer:

Father, I thank You that restoration belongs to me through the blood of Your Son, Jesus! I thank You that I am well, healed, healthy and whole inside and out! I patiently await the fullness of Your promise yet to manifest in my life! Praise God!

Notes

CHAPTER 21

Who's Right and Who's Wrong?

Age-Old Question:

Aaahhhh, the age-old marital debate of, *"Who is right and who is wrong?"* This question baffles the wisest scholars. There will be differing opinions within marriage, no matter how great the marriage. Questions will arise about how to raise children, whether to have children or how many, where to attend church, how to vote, friends, children's friends, finances, organize or decorate the home, what state, city, town, or street to reside, and a bottomless pit of other issues from minuscule to life-altering. With these questions, conflict can easily erupt.

In general, a significant issue is, *"That's the way my parents did it, so your way must be wrong."* It's hard to fathom just how petty people who supposedly love each other can become. My parents, who have been married nearly sixty years, used to fight over how and when to wash the dishes, clean the house, balance a checkbook, and more. No two households are run the same. This leaves newlyweds in absolute turmoil if not nipped in the bud before marriage. Most people believe the only way to accomplish even the most medial task is to do it precisely the way their parents did it. These hot topics should be resolved prior to standing at the altar. Compromise with an open mind about how things are accomplished day-to-day is necessary. Issues will always arise throughout the best of marriages, but learning how to work through them as soon as possible is crucial.

The upside to being married three times is having gleaned much knowledge about conflict resolution. One main lesson is simply that most things are not worth the fallout of engaging in a battle. Since indoor plumbing was invented, a big issue with women is men refusing to change the toilet paper roll. It sounds silly, but it can be the straw that breaks the camel's back, to be sure. Then there's not putting down the toilet seat. Again, sounds insignificant but can altogether be the cause of a huge fight, one that could easily lead to divorce court if you're not on your spiritual toes.

When there is current turmoil, underlying though it may be, between the husband and wife, it takes something very minor to spark a fight when it really isn't the issue at all. We must learn to pick our battles just with parents raising their children. We need to learn to communicate with open, honest calm. In the next chapter, we'll go into more detail about communicating one to another in a healthy fashion. For this topic, we'll stick to when and where we should have an open discussion about disagreements and how to discern what is worth a discussion.

Commonly in young marriages, the first year is the most difficult because the two are not used to sharing—and sharing everything! Although the married couple consists of two adults, sharing is a well-known topic for parents raising toddlers and teens. A friend told me that when she and her husband first married, she became filled with anger over him eating her candy bars. She said they had a knock-down, drag-out fight over them. I'm both amazed and amused at what can trigger such a response, yet the tent in which we reside is greedy by nature, not to mention selfish to the core.

Humans want what we want, when we want it, and how we want it, and God forbid someone should mess with our routine. Those candy bars were hers, and he had no right to take them without permission, at least in her mind!

Everyone wants to believe they are always right in every scenario, no matter how much of a *"good person"* they think themselves to be. Here's the thing. If we choose to put other people's needs before our own, squabbles would never happen. We are called to love our spouse as our own body. The problem enters when one or both refuse to ever concede. For centuries, there's been the running joke that men should always nod their heads in agreement with their wife, that the wife is always right. That's cute, but that way of thinking will cause animosity to erect on a foundation of anger. No one should or could possibly always be right or wrong. That is grossly imbalanced, and imbalance causes things to crumble to the ground.

No Longer an Individual:

The truth is that we need to recognize we are no longer individuals but joined as one entity with our polar opposite. It is never right to think, *"I'm right—always. They should always apologize to me."* Humility is required for any healthy, godly marriage, just as in our intimate walk with God. Humility and God's pure love go hand-in-hand.

> Do nothing from selfishness or empty conceit, but with humility of mind regard one another as more important than yourselves; do not merely look out for your own personal interests, but also for the interests of others. Have this attitude in yourselves which was also in Christ Jesus, who, although He existed in the form of God, did not regard equality with God a thing to be grasped, but emptied Himself, taking the form of a bond-servant, and being made in the likeness of men. Being found in appearance as a man, He humbled

Himself by becoming obedient to the point of death, even death on a cross (Philippians 2:3-8).

A bond-servant is defined as *"devoted to another to the disregard of one's own interests."* If Christ, who is God, came to lowly Earth He created to save sinful man He created by dying on a cross for sin He did not commit, all for the sake of saving the ones He loved that didn't love Him, how much more should we who say we love our spouse—with whom we have become one being—love them in this way? Aren't we called to humble ourselves for the sake of the greater good? Jesus did not regard equality with God as an attainable thing even though He was God in human form. In this attitude of complete humility, He emptied Himself becoming a bond-servant.

The text also reads, *"…do not merely look out for your own personal interests, but also for the interests of others."* This does not say, *"never look out for your own interests."* While you do have your own interests, always take the other person's into consideration, or rather, in addition. Some people like to take the Word of God and twist it to their personal advantage. Those same people would try to lord this over their spouse in an attempt to *"always"*—there's that word again—get their own selfish way.

Imagine a world where every married couple looked out for the other first. What a beautiful world that would be! No one would be greedy for their own desires. When everyone is giving and selfless, as was Christ, everyone would have what they need. Sadly, most people are inconsiderate, selfish, greedy, self-seeking, and constantly picking apart their spouses and looking for the negative. This selfish mindset and attitude are as much against God's will as any other sin. How is the matrimony holy when marriages stay together based on such evil?

When we love someone the way Christ loves His people, then we have the chance for a genuinely successful marriage. That is a love entirely designed by God for marriage, our spiritual marriage to

God, and our spiritual and physical marriage to our earthly spouse. If, however, our motive for marriage was and is not the love of God, we will find it vastly challenging to humble ourselves before them in a time of disagreement. In fact, if Christ's love is not at the root of our marriage, we will find ourselves in constant conflict and competing to *"win"* every dispute. We may even go so far as to pick a fight just for the sake of being able to conquer it.

Neither Are Right: Submission Required:

Honestly, the answer to the original question of who is right or wrong can be answered and resolved by completely submitting our hearts to Jesus Christ. Nothing in this life, marriage or anything else, will be truly successful and fruitful unless we choose to surrender to Christ first. If we are merely *"doing the Christian or church thing"* out of routine or what we've been taught is right, our heart is not in it, and we will not be able to forfeit a *"win"* without bitterness rooting in our hearts and growing a tree of disdain, hatred, and unforgiveness against our spouse. Remember from an earlier discussion that God calls us to *"surrender,"* not *"commitment."* Commitment, which is you in control instead of God, causes one to become bitter in *"doing right."* Mere commitment drives pride in all of our *"doing right,"* leading the person to think of themselves as better than their spouse. Surrender always leads to selflessness and humility.

There is a place that exists in our spirit-man where we can let our spouse *"win one"* without becoming resentful feeling like a doormat or pushover. That place is where we willingly submit to the greater good of Christ, and our spirit is connecting to Holy Spirit on a day-to-day basis. Otherwise, even if we relent and forfeit being right, we'll begin harboring anger against our spouse because they *"never let me win."*

On the other hand, God's people individually and collectively begin to seek His face, heart, and will in everything, our hearts toward our spouses will change. Humility is a requirement for

God's blessings, and humility comes exclusively from God. Without humility, marriage doesn't stand much of a chance of flourishing as God intends. Just because a marriage doesn't end in divorce does not equate success. I know far too many marriages that *"lasted,"* yet they were both completely miserable.

Once we begin seeing our spouse through God's single vision, we will no longer ask the age-old question, W*ho is right and who is wrong?"* We will only seek to be in right standing with God [holy, acceptable, and obedient to His perfect will]. Once we obtain a clear picture of a couple being *"one new creation,"* we'll realize neither can always be correct or incorrect. There remains only one entity void of separation. Conflict divides our *"kingdom"* because, as the Scripture states in Matthew 12:25, *"Every kingdom divided against itself will be ruined, and every city or household divided against itself will not stand."* The question becomes obsolete because we view the two individuals only as one kingdom, one undivided unit.

It's only when we perpetually see ourselves as individuals within a marriage that we seek to be *"right"* and prove them wrong. This perspective is fleshly, carnal, and against God, because it is set against the union we chose to enter.

> "Pride goes before destruction, and a haughty spirit before stumbling. It is better to be humble in spirit with the lowly than to divide the spoil with the proud (Proverbs 16:18-19)."

If we are looking to destroy our marriages, operate in pride. If we want to divide our household [kingdom], allow pride to rule our hearts. I love the above text in Proverbs. It is well known but not well heeded. A person's humble spirit will fare far better through this life than one self-seeking, self-serving, self-glorifying—or in other words, one who always needs to be recognized as *"right."* I'll end this chapter with a section from *What Was God Thinking?* chapter five, *"The Root of the Problem."* You may find it of interest for your marriage or future marriage:

Current Problems Rooted in Eden:

> "When the woman saw that the tree was good for food, and that it was a delight to the eyes, and that the tree was desirable to make one wise, she took from its fruit and ate; and she gave also to her husband with her, and he ate (Genesis 3:6)."

Herein lays the problem of most people throughout the generations. First, man had the role of guarding the garden and everything in it. By deferring to the woman, he not only gave over his authority to Satan, but he also gave his authoritative role to the woman. This was a blatant recalcitrant [rebellious] act against God. Even now, women struggle with men's complacency. Because Adam was complacent in his leadership role over his domain, men struggle with women dominating them.

Because God gave Adam authority and Adam gave it back to Lucifer through the sin act, mankind's flesh was cursed by God. The flesh [the fleshly nature] needs to be treated as though it is defiled and dead—irreversibly cursed. Through the blood of the Lamb, anyone can be transformed from the natural of Earth to the supernatural of Heaven. People need to bring the old Adamic fleshly nature in repentance before God to break the yoke of death, no matter how *"good"* you believe yourself to be. Though the body appears alive, without Christ, it is the walking dead.

Understanding Submission:

> Submitting yourselves one to another in the fear of God…Wives, be subject to your husbands, as to the

Lord. For the husband is the head of the wife, as Christ also is the head of the church, He Himself being the Savior of the body. But as the church is subject to Christ, so also the wives ought to be to their husbands in everything. Husbands, love your wives, as Christ also loved the church and gave Himself up for her, so that He might sanctify her, having cleansed her by the washing of water with the word, that He might present to Himself the church in all her glory, having no spot or wrinkle or any such thing; but that she would be holy and blameless. So husbands ought also to love their wives as their bodies. He who loves his wife loves himself (Ephesians 5:21, 22-28, KJV).

"But Christ has rescued us from the curse pronounced by the law. When He was hung on the cross, He took upon Himself the curse for our wrongdoing. For it is written in the Scriptures, 'Cursed is everyone who is hung on a tree (Galatians 3:13, NLT).'"

Definition of Submission: the action or fact of accepting or yielding to a superior force or to the will or authority of another person.

Adam's place was to say, "*No*" to Eve and lovingly direct her to say, "*No*" to the enemy. This is why women, generally speaking, set the standard in relationships with men, whether spiritual, sexual, financial, or other. Adam allowed the woman to set the standard, therefore, so it is today. We must break this cycle from homes. Of necessity, the rightful role of authority must be handed back to the husband by the wife, and the husband needs to hand authority back to Christ. In this, both the husband and the wife are in proper alignment with Holy Spirit, and peace will rule.

When done correctly, the woman will no longer have to run things. She will become her husband's helper. Neither will have to dominate the other as they will operate in their God-ordained role. They will live harmoniously instead of nearly killing one another with poor attitudes, harsh words, or devastating silence. They will better handle difficulties and disagreements.

The Body of Christ is instructed that the wife is to submit to her husband, but equally, the husband is to submit to God. We are also instructed to *"submit one to another"* so that the greater good of God's Kingdom will manifest. Because of Adam and Eve's rebellion, the power-struggle continues to this day. No one wants to humble themselves one to another; wife to husband, husband to wife, both to God. Imagine a world where both people in marriage were so set on pleasing Yahweh that humility reigned. Wow! Neither would ever have to beg, whine, or use controlling manipulation. When we can get to the root of any problem, we can resolve it. My friend and ministry partner, Sandy Renner, defines wisdom as the ability to apply the solution to the problem.

There is a looming curse over women dating back to Eve, as we see in Genesis 3:6. Just as Adam gave up authority to Eve, Eve sought to possess authority so much that she didn't want Adam's authority or God's. This way, she brought a controlling, manipulative, evil spirit upon women. Women worldwide nag their husbands to step up to the proverbial plate, but when he finally decides to do so, the wife often resists.

Women have an innate desire to control, coerce, and manipulate. Many women say, *"You need to be a man and take charge,"* yet actions speak a very different message. Wives need to allow husbands to make decisions even if it means letting them make mistakes along the way. Women with sons, teach them how to be men of God. It's time to relinquish headship to the husbands, and husbands give headship to Christ.

Women are to submit, not control. Men are to love their wives as Christ loves the Church, not control. This will lead both to submit one to another because they are submitting first to Christ. With this understanding, the lack of Holy Spirit leading in Adam, Eve, and the modern-day Christ-follower makes it easy to recognize how the problem escalated over time. Since Jesus bore the curse of the fleshly nature for all mankind, by properly applying His blood, there's no reason to continue in Adam and Eve's footsteps.

Once we begin to seek first the Kingdom of God, we'll start to delve into the Kingdom Constitution [Bible] desiring, most earnestly, to pledge our allegiance to the King, His Kingdom, and His edicts. Submission will no longer be an impossibility, but altogether supernaturally natural. (end excerpt)

Prayer:

Father, may the very humility that Jesus Christ walked in as a perfect human being dwell richly within me. I surrender my prideful flesh to You today and every day. Remind me that it is by the grace of the One who did not deserve to die, that I have any life at all. Selah.

Notes

CHAPTER 22

Know Your Position

You're *Not* the Child:

It would behoove us all to remember we are not our spouse's child, sibling, or parent. Any person can digress into a childish state mentally and/or emotionally. Especially in younger married people where one or both had an unhealthy relationship with their parents. If a woman was used to her daddy constantly scolding her, not allowing her to make a sound decision on her own, she might continue that pattern well into her marriage. In like manner, if a man was used to his mother coddling and doing everything for him, he may easily expect his wife to mother him. Rest assured neither scenario is healthy.

Within marriage, men should be men, and women should be women. They are equal in decision-making and nurturing one another, assisting their growth in every capacity. If you find yourself in a situation where your husband is playing *"Daddy,"* or your wife is playing *"Mommy,"* have a candid discussion. Speak to one another confidently, securely, and plainly so as not to leave things open for interpretation. If you need outside help, find a godly counselor to help you through this unhealthy phase. Both will likely need to get to the root causing them to parent or be parented—each feeds negatively off the other.

You're *Not* a Sibling:

Never, under any circumstance, treat your spouse like a brother or sister. I know a couple that had a disagreement. The wife scolded her husband about something he did, screaming, "*I told my mom!*" "*What, you told your mom? Why would you do that?*" he replied in a panic realizing she snitched on him! This is most definitely not a healthy relationship.

Tattling to your parents, in-laws, friends, or whomever is not the way to handle difficulty. This same wife constantly treats her husband as her child or brother. She is bossy, demanding of his time, and spies waiting for his next wrong move. He is a bit lazy and sloppy, and she's a neat freak. She's constantly nagging about what he does wrong. Often, the way we treat a child or sibling is the same way we engage with a spouse. This should not be.

Women, You Are *Not* His Mommy:

"Love does no harm to its neighbor. Therefore love is the fulfillment of the Law (Romans 13:10)."

"With all humility and gentleness, with patience, bearing with one another in love, eager to maintain the unity of the Spirit in the bond of peace (Ephesians 4:2-3)."

"Complete my joy by being of the same mind, having the same love, being in full accord and of one mind (Philippians 2:2)."

So many times, especially with women, it's easy to go into "*mommy mode*" without realizing it. Mommy mode is the automatic reflex wanting to "*train*" instead of "*walk beside.*" Unfortunately, it's the worst place to be. As women, we're hardwired to teach and to train children since we are the ones God created to bear children.

If a woman is faced with her husband's pornography addiction, as was I with Michael, because his bad habit was so insulting, grotesque, and altogether repulsive to me, automatically, I wanted to be "*Mommy*" informing him how horrible it is and he shouldn't indulge. Although what I said was accurate, my approach left him feeling smaller and smaller without hope of regaining his manhood in my eyes. Mommy-mode must be left to raising children and should never be applied to husbands. Some men go into daddy-mode wanting to raise their wives instead of standing beside them.

Do not mother your husband as it is harmful to him and very unhealthy. Love him, ladies—love him, support him, encourage him, stand beside him when he does something incorrect and possibly completely stupid—unless, of course, you desire to live in a miserable marriage or divorce. For any successful marriage, you must seek God's wisdom about how to speak to and treat your husband with courtesy in the worst of situations. I believe I've mentioned that if your husband is physically abusing or hurting you in a life-threatening way, get out. Seek help and then reevaluate once you're in a safe environment. Outside of physical, mental, or emotional harm, learn God's perspective on what true love is. After all, you did sign the dotted line and vowing to love through better or worse.

Men, You Are *Not* Her Daddy:

Men often treat their wives as their daughters. They want to punish for "*bad*" behavior or not "*obeying*" their commands. This should never be. Just as a woman need not "*mommy*" their husbands, men should not belittle their wives treating them as inferior or ignorant children. Men must treat their wives with respect and equality in marriage. They should definitely never misuse the Scripture, "*wives, submit to your husband*" found in Ephesians 5:22-23.

Too many times, I've heard of such abuse. Men, in this respect, enjoy taking God's words and twisting them until they're unrecognizable. Husbands and wives are not to be each other's parents in any capacity. We are not positioned to raise our spouse but to grow together in grace, love, and honor.

It Isn't Your Job to Change Your Spouse:

> "Above all, love each other deeply, because love covers a multitude of sins (I Peter 4:8)."

> "Hatred stirs dissension, but love covers over all wrongs (Proverbs 10:2)."

If we could only recognize the simple fact that it is not our job or right to change our spouse. Love never dictates changing people but instead loving them through their awkward phases and/or habits until they choose a better way. We married them, so there must have been some redeeming quality before we arrived at *"They are driving me crazy!"* Never, never, never enter a marriage expecting to change your spouse as that is foolish on its best day!

Again, when Michael and I were dealing with the pornography habit he'd practiced since his teen years, as did all the men in his home, I had to realize that no matter how horrible I viewed it, it was not my lot in life to make him change. With this knowledge, I was freed from the pressure of trying to *"fix"* him. The Bible says that only God can change the heart of a king (Proverbs 21:1) and, with this simple knowledge, we can release our husbands or wives to God leaving it to Him to do necessary changing. Love is a funny thing because it remains through and through when it's from God. It's ingrained in us no matter what offense stems from the one we love.

God is love. He created mankind. Mankind rejected Him, destroying the Earth He created. Because of His undying, unwavering love, He sent His Son to die for those He created as well as give us

His entire Kingdom we, most assuredly, do not deserve. Real love cannot be removed, replaced, or faded. In such love, you will choose to respond with kindness, mercy, and grace desiring to help, not change. God's love through us will cause the person to desire change. Michael had fallen back into pornography in 2015 after God initially exposed his addiction in 2008. I continued loving him through it, just as he loves me through my misgivings. Love covers a multitude of sins, which brings us to the next section on punishment.

Punishment is *Not* the Answer:

> "There is no fear in love. But perfect love drives out fear, because fear has to do with punishment. The one who fears is not made perfect in love. We love because He first loved us (I John 4:18-19)."

> "For judgment will be merciless to one who has shown no mercy; mercy triumphs over judgment (James 2:13)."

> "Each one of you also must love his wife as he loves himself, and the wife must respect her husband (Ephesians 5:33)."

A punishment mentality often stems from parenting, which is also an incorrect perspective. As a parent, we should see as does God, which means we don't seek to punish but to discipline. The difference is that punishment is merciless and stems from condemnation and fear. However, discipline is merciful in so much as it leads one into self-discipline to become better. It blossoms from a deep heart of love.

God's love is so eternal that when He sent Jesus to die for our sins and rise from the dead, He brought all of mankind into a place of rest, grace, and mercy. God no longer rules in punishment, at least not until after gathering His bride. We live in a day where mercy trumps judgment; therefore, punishment is not

God's way currently. Why do we think punishment should be our way if it is not God's?

In marriage, you are one with your spouse. Since you are one, you punish yourself if you punish your husband or wife. There are all kinds of punishments people inflict upon their wayward spouse. They withhold sex, money, time, cooking, cleaning, communication, or anything that would goad them. As a general rule, people love punishment; unless, of course, it's a punishment against themselves. Punishment is the opposite of love, grace, and mercy.

I love James 2:13, which states boldly, *"For judgment will be merciless to one who has shown no mercy."* I don't believe married folks generally apply this Scripture to themselves, but we all should. If there were more mercy, there'd be fewer divorces, and that's just a simple truth. It's so effortless to be merciless with the Word of God, such as, *"The Bible says adultery is a cause for divorce"* therefore, they move right into divorce without extending God's supernatural love, mercy, or grace. In fact, many couples that divorce don't want a divorce, but because they're in *"punishment mode,"* they go forward to punish their spouse. In turn, everyone suffers, so what good was their punishment since no one changed for the better?

Don't go into punishment autopilot when something goes wrong within your marriage. You are one singular entity. If you hurt your spouse, you hurt yourself. If you punish them, you punish yourself. If you have anger to express, wait until you've calmed, and then express your disappointment and irritation in a way that will help the marriage instead of further hinder it. For your own sake, I implore you to heed these words if you want a healthy, thriving, lasting marriage. Unify, don't separate. Don't parent your spouse. Love them. Don't try to change them. Love them. Don't punish them. Love them because love makes all the difference in the world!

Prayer:

Father, I surrender my marriage, attitude, anger, disappointment, judgment, and life to You. Thank You for displaying and extending Your supernatural, eternal, unfailing love toward me personally, and I ask that You stir within me that same love that comes only from above so that I will walk, talk, eat, drink, and breath that love in my marriage. Help me to love my spouse as You love me. Allow me to think before I speak and never act in anger. Teach me Your ways, O Lord, that I will always give mercy instead of punishment, grace instead of malice, love instead of hatred. Show me Your love so that I can first receive it for myself and then grant such eternal love toward my spouse as an extension of myself. Fill me with Your love and give me eyes to see as You see, ears to hear as You hear, and a mind to understand and process as do You. I love You, Yeshua, and I thank You for my marriage. Rule this marriage through me lest I make a huge mess. Selah.

Notes

CHAPTER 23

Healthy Communication

Love is patient, love is kind and is not jealous; love does not brag and is not arrogant, does not act unbecomingly; it does not seek its own, is not provoked, does not take into account a wrong suffered, does not rejoice in unrighteousness, but rejoices with the truth; bears all things, believes all things, hopes all things, endures all things. Love never fails (I Corinthians 13:4-8).

Love is Patient, Love is Kind:

When one thinks of love, we often think of the superficial benefits of being loved by another. I'd like to open this chapter with a well-known set of verses in I Corinthians. They are quoted endlessly, yet I see very few people actually walking in genuine love.

In marriage, when we truly love our spouse, we will be patient and kind, never jealous, braggadocios, or prideful. We will not be rude, self-seeking, or easily provoked by things that irritate us. We will be forgiving and lay the matter to rest. We will not delight in wrongdoing and always delight in the truth, even if it is painful to acknowledge. We will bear the burden of our spouse, no matter the weight. We will believe in what God is accomplishing whether we can see it yet or not; we will hope in the love Christ promised no matter how dark the days, and we will endure 'til the end. Our love will not fail if it is Christ's, supernatural love.

One of the most troublesome marriage areas lies in communication or the lack thereof. Time and time again, I hear the same thing from wives, "*He just doesn't listen to me. No matter what I say, it's as though I'm speaking a foreign language.*" And from the husbands, I hear, "*She just won't stop talking! Nag, nag, nag, whine, whine, whine; talk, talk, talk; that's all she wants to do. Every little feeling she experiences, she needs to express them.*" Can anyone see the problem?

The question is discovering the answer to, "*How can a couple seeking a healthy marriage remedy the problem?*" Men and women definitely do not think the same way because we're not designed to—we're wired differently. Men need to learn to listen to her words and hear the message. On the other hand, women need to discover how to filter their words, saying only that which will bring positive results and not go on and on endlessly about mundane issues and every minor irritation.

Reading and Interpreting the Signs:

In my first marriage, my husband didn't love me. At the time, I didn't understand that was the core problem. He always shut me out. Attempting to make him communicate, I would speak louder and louder as if this would somehow prod him. My method was unproductive; not only unproductive, but it intensified the situation. Once he did speak, he told me things like, "You *talk too much. You embarrass me. Be quiet!*" My first marriage was a ruse from the start, so it's a pretty bad scenario to use in conflict resolution. However, in my current marriage, we are in love with one another. I am a vocal person, and he is reticent. Many times I would ask, "*Don't you have anything to say? Don't you want to talk?*" As you may guess, "*No*" was his response. He said that if he had something to say, he'd have already said it. Makes sense, right?

I learned early that his silence was not a sign of lovelessness, as was my first husband's. Every situation is different; therefore, there is no exact science on how to communicate well from one marriage to the next. I can only make suggestions that work for me by sharing my personal experiences of things I did right and wrong and that I have heard through others and what they have experienced.

Michael and I were friends long before we married, so that helps a great deal. I do recommend that people develop a strong friendship prior to marriage. When people skip this step, it causes a great deal more problems needing ironing post-marriage. Before the wedding, we casually talked about ground rules. We agreed that if either of us ever wanted out, we'd be open and honest—up front about it instead of ducking behind dark corners trying to hide truth. Also, if either of us developed a crush on someone, we'd discuss that and move through it together.

That may sound ridiculous, but admit it or not, crushes happen. When left unspoken and unchecked, that can lead down a very dark and destructive path leaving far more problems to trudge through than just admitting to the initial crush. To be certain, when the couple is mature and secure in their love and conviction to honoring the marital covenant, they will willingly hear something as painful as this so they can confront it as a *united front* as one unit instead of as two individuals. It's only when we hide inner feelings that a volcanic eruption is imminent.

Marriage of Freedom, Not Bondage:

It was for freedom that Christ set us free; therefore keep standing firm and do not be subject again to a yoke of slavery...For you were called to freedom, brethren; only do not turn your freedom into an opportunity for the flesh, but through love serve one another. For the whole Law is fulfilled in one word, in the statement, "YOU SHALL LOVE YOUR NEIGHBOR AS YOURSELF." But if you bite and devour one another, take care that you are not consumed by one another. But I say, walk by the Spirit, and you will not carry out the desire of the flesh. For the flesh sets its desire against the Spirit, and the Spirit against the flesh; for these are in opposition to one another, so that you may not do the things that you please. But if you are led by the Spirit, you are not under the Law. Now the deeds of the flesh are evident, which are: immorality, impurity, sensuality, idolatry, sorcery, enmities, strife, jealousy, outbursts of anger, disputes, dissensions, factions, envying, drunkenness, carousing, and things like these, of which I forewarn you, just as I have forewarned you, that those who practice such things will not inherit the Kingdom of God. But the fruit of the Spirit is love, joy, peace, patience, kindness, goodness, faithfulness, gentleness, self-control; against such things there is no law. Now those who belong to Christ Jesus have crucified the flesh with its passions and desires (Galatians 5:1, 13-24).

Marriage should be a place of freedom, never bondage. When the purest form of love is present and is our daily pursuit, the ways of the fleshly man will be brought into subjection to Jesus before we allow it to move us to action. Take a close look at what Yahweh tells us is of the flesh [sin driven]: immorality, impurity, sensuality, idolatry [anything centered around self], sorcery [witchcraft, manipulation, control], enmities [hatred between enemies], strife, jealousy [covet, resent, distrust), outbursts of anger, disputes [to question, struggle, oppose], dissensions [disagreement, conflict], factions [conflict], envying [wanting what belongs to another], drunkenness, carousing [drink and become noisy].

These are significant issues that occur frequently within marriages. Look at how many times YHWH uses a word meaning basically the same thing—enmity, strife, dispute, faction, dissension—they all produce fighting. These are what married couples must avoid. The only way to prevent such ungodly behavior is to seek resolution, not making your spouse feel bad about themselves but to comfort and encourage.

More often than not, we enter a debate with our spouses, not to resolve an issue but to let them know how right we are. We become so prideful that we refuse to release a simple and insignificant problem. We feel we must *"win the fight"* so we stop seeing our spouses as one with us and begin seeing them as the opposing team [our personal enemy separate and disconnected from us]. This is a ploy from the real enemy to destroy everything—our walk with God, marriage, children, ministry, and testimony. It's time to awaken to God's perspective, hearing, thinking, doing, and lay self and pride in the grave where they belong.

Why, oh why, would we purpose to hurt the very person we willingly gave ourselves? It is mind-boggling when we really stop to think of what we're doing. Again, this is one of the many reasons we must seek God's face before entering marital covenant lest we find ourselves in woeful regret.

Ladies, absolutely do not marry someone you cannot respect. Men, absolutely do not marry someone you can't love regardless of weight gain or her ability to perform sexually. The husband is the head of the home—if we choose to put the wrong man in such a position of authority, we need look no further than the mirror to place blame. Men, the woman is to be cherished above all else in your life, including your mother, friends, hobbies, and your career— if you find yourself struggling with that, look no further than the mirror.

Healthy communication within the marriage begins before marriage. If our communication is unhealthy prior to marriage, we can expect the issue only to intensify. Marriage is often viewed by the naïve as a *"fix-all"* to their existing problems; however, the opposite is true. If we can't properly communicate while dating or engaged, pump the breaks! If both are unwilling to abstain from sex before marriage, pump the breaks. If both parties can't agree on how to raise children, who, where, or how long one should or should not work, how to maturely communicate and resolve issues, please be wise and courageous enough to say, *"This isn't going to work."* If all you do is fight and disagree—well, you get the picture.

Marriage can be difficult enough when two people are designed by God for one another, much less dragging low expectations into it. May we all begin, single or married, to seek God's face, heart, mind, and will to become consumed by His unfailing, supernatural love.

Notes

CHAPTER 24

What's Yours is Mine

"Above all, keep fervent in your love for *one another*, because love covers a multitude of sins (I Peter 4:8)."

"Honor your father and mother (which is the first commandment with a promise) (Ephesians 6:2)."

Your Parents are My Parents?!

Every newly married couple must know that whatever is his becomes hers and vice versa. As great as that sounds, it is all-inclusive, bar nothing! In-laws are a big deal, and they can often be a deal-breaker. A spouse's family can be the single most troublesome issue in any marriage. One set of in-laws is receptive and respectful. The other is commonly the direct opposite. Whether anyone likes to admit it or not, generally speaking, mothers of sons are much more likely to be a problem than mothers of daughters. However, fathers of daughters are more likely to be a problem than fathers of sons; it's simple math. I have spoken with hundreds of couples, and rarely is the opposite true, though there are exceptions to every rule.

Whenever I conduct premarital counseling, I make sure they understand one simple truth. Where the Scripture reads, "*they shall be-*

come one flesh," it means there is no difference between his parents and her parents, his money and her money, his property, her property, and so on. Accepting this as an absolute, especially concerning in-laws, is a most difficult reality to face. They must view the fiancé's parents as soon-to-be equally their own parents. When each person grasps this concept, it lends to greater levels of respect and not losing their cool when an issue surrounding them arises. This is the only way I have personally been able to successfully respect my in-laws no matter the situation. If I would not speak to my flesh and blood parents disrespectfully, I refuse, no matter how tempting, to talk to my husband's parents disrespectfully. To do anything less is to disobey the commandment of God to *"honor your father and mother"* and inadvertently block our own blessings.

I highly recommend that, when there is a conflict with the spouse's parents that needs handling, she should deal with hers, and he should deal with his. Unfortunately, men—again, I'm general-ly speaking—have much more difficulty confronting their parents than the woman has facing hers. If the potential husband could understand just how imperative it is that he never choose his mother over his wife, the marriage has a greater chance of not only surviv-ing but thriving. Vice versa applies to the soon-to-be wife.

Michael and I agreed before marriage that I would never have to defend myself to his family or him to mine. There must be bound-aries. For every couple believing God's Word and purposing to be obedient, love must be first and foremost above all else—within the marriage for each other, but also toward family. Even if we must distance ourselves from either set of parents, love must be applied and restoration the ultimate goal.

When we see our in-laws as *"my spouse's family,"* we miss the mark. However, when we choose to see them as God intended, everything changes—more specifically, our attitudes, words, and actions. We are to honor our in-laws as our own flesh and blood parents.

My Situation:

I'll share my story for a more personal application. I use my own situation to help you see that this isn't only possible when the in-laws like and love you, but it is altogether possible when they dislike you and even go so far as to hate you.

I have been around my husband's family since 1983, beginning with being friends with one of his female cousins a year or two before realizing they were related or even knew one another. I was close to her parents and knew her family. Michael's parents would sometimes be there when I would visit her parents. Technically, though I didn't know them intimately, we were acquainted.

After sixteen years passed, his cousin and I had a falling out. To my sorrow, in my anger and hurt, I wrote a lengthy letter that was quite vivid and spiteful. For your information, this was during my time of rebellion against God. Because of this, what should have been between two people became a family feud, including Michael's mother. Most of the things my soon-to-be mother-in-law perceived of me were not true, and what was true was blown way out of proportion. There are far too many details to share, but I'll give a brief overview. The first ten years she knew of me, to my knowledge, she neither liked nor disliked me. For the following nineteen years, she did not like me for reasons unknown. For the latter fourteen of those nineteen years, she used my rift with his cousin—her niece—as an excuse to fuel her growing disdain.

Needless to say, there were many occasions where the fleshly part of me wanted to retaliate verbally with sarcasm and insults. Believe me when I say that confrontation comes very easily to my natural man! Because I daily allowed Holy Spirit to reign as my life—not simply *"in"* my life—I always pulled back, taking the necessary time to repent of my judgment against her, forgive her actions against me, and refresh myself with God's ways, mind, and will.

I must admit that was not always an easy task. Truth be told, I can't remember when it was ever easy. This woman who became my mother by law was nothing like my biological mother, nothing like anything familiar or relatable to me. I didn't understand her, and she didn't understand me. Throw in false accusations into an already uncomfortable situation, and chaos ensued!

I desperately wanted to be a daughter to her, to just love her without conflict. Sadly, there was exceeding conflict, to my spiritual growth and benefit. It was, for me, like fighting an already lost cause, and, on many occasions, it all seemed pointless. She absolutely desecrated my name to her family and my father-in-law's family, to those who knew me and had never met me. Knowing merely a fraction of the vile things of which she accused me made it nearly unbearable to be around her.

Case in point, she loved Christmas, and she did it exceptionally well. Her decorations were unmatched. It was the one time of year when her three sons would come home and be together. One year, I had kidney stones and was in considerable pain. We drove an hour to her house because I didn't want to ruin her Christmas. Our daughters, Sophia and Geni, were little at that time, and I didn't want them to miss out. Geni is our daughter we brought into our home at birth, and we raised her alongside Sophia; they are only six months apart. Geni is of a different race. Michael's brother brought his girlfriend—we had not met previously. The day went as well as possible, given my level of discomfort.

The following Easter, we went to visit. My mother-in-law proceeded berating me in front of Michael and his dad, expressing how I *"ruined her Christmas."* She accused me of snubbing the brother's girlfriend because, and I quote, *"You were wearing brand new shoes, and she was wearing old sloppy shoes. I saw the way you looked at her. I was watching you the whole day!"*

Needless to say, we couldn't have been more surprised by this encounter. This went on for well over an hour. Part of the conversation was about Geni and her ethnicity. At that point, Michael stood up, excused us, and we went home. The fact that neither of us told her off right then and there was a miracle from God! It took every fiber of my being not to do so. While she was steadily insulting me, I talked to Holy Spirit internally.

That conversation put a wedge between us for a few years. I even wrote a letter expressing my love for her, but until she was ready to receive my love, I would not continuously put myself in her path of rejection; whenever she was ready, I was here for her. Soon after that, we received news that she told the whole family, "*Alexys sent me a letter just like the letter she sent her* [Michael's cousin]." They were nothing alike.

Blessed are the Peacemakers:

This is just one of the countless examples of the whirlwind of torment I experienced with this woman, now my mother. I didn't know what to do with or about her. I didn't know how to treat someone who not only hated me but simply did not love or like me. Talk about a spiritual challenge! May I say, though, it is not our loved ones who grow and stretch us spiritually, but our enemies. My mother-in-law—an enemy by her choice—taught me far more than anyone else could about how to fully apply what I preach and teach. She was an instrument from God in my life to teach me how to properly and willingly use the following commands of God:

> But I say to you who hear, love your enemies, do good to those who hate you, bless those who curse you, pray for those who mistreat you. Whoever hits you on the cheek, offer him the other also; and whoever takes away your coat, do not withhold your shirt from him either. Give to everyone who asks of you, and whoever takes away what is yours, do not demand it back. Treat others the same way you want them to treat you. If you love those who love you, what credit is that to you? For even sinners love those who love them. If you do good to those who do good to you, what credit is that to you? For

even sinners do the same. If you lend to those from whom you expect to receive, what credit is that to you? Even sinners lend to sinners in order to receive back the same amount. But love your enemies, and do good, and lend, expecting nothing in return; and your reward will be great, and you will be sons of the Most High; for He Himself is kind to ungrateful and evil men. Be merciful, just as your Father is merciful. Do not judge, and you will not be judged; and do not condemn, and you will not be condemned; pardon, and you will be pardoned. Give, and it will be given to you. They will pour into your lap a good measure—pressed down, shaken together, and running over. For by your standard of measure it will be measured to you in return (Luke 6:27-38).

Blessed are the peacemakers, for they will be called children of God. Blessed are those who are persecuted because of righteousness, for theirs is the Kingdom of Heaven. Blessed are you when people insult you, persecute you and falsely say all kinds of evil against you because of Me. rejoice and be glad, because great is your reward in Heaven, for in the same way they persecuted the prophets who were before you (Matthew 5:9-12).

This comes back to understanding that the flesh is constantly at war with God's Spirit within. I always chose love no matter what; to love her as my own mother. This allowed me to treat her with respect faster than if I viewed her simply as *"Michael's mother."* When we keep God's mind as our own, it keeps the fleshly mind at bay, though ever-present.

Many events transpired over the years, leaving me pulling down from my mind and heart my own hatred and allowing God to restore me into His perfect love. I would not let myself retain such animosity, though I could have easily justified it with my natural man. Although I was by no means perfect, I purposed to never raise my voice or disrespect her in any way. The greatest lesson for me was learning how to accept that there are certain people I can never love in my natural state. I had to humble myself before God completely, admit my fleshly inability, and allow Him to express His supernatural love through me. Therefore, it wasn't I who loved her, but He who is within me.

In this, I gave her no justification to rightly say, *"See, I told you I was right about her."* I purposed to keep my testimony intact against the will of my fleshly man as Peter instructs us in I Peter 3:16, stating, *"and keep a good conscience so that in the thing in which you are slandered, those who revile your good behavior in Christ will be put to shame."* Paul also gives similar instruction in Romans 16:16-17, instructing, *"Therefore do not let what is for you a good thing be spoken of as evil; for the Kingdom of God is not eating and drinking, but righteousness and peace and joy in the Holy Spirit."*

Worth the Wait:

Fast forward to July 2012, my mother-in-law was diagnosed with terminal cancer. In an odd turn of events, to say the least, I was the first person she called to tell her distressful news. I missed her initial call and could not return it for three hours. She broke the news to me first citing she refused to tell another soul, including her sister, until she spoke to me. I could not have been more shocked, both by her news and her desire to tell only me. That spoke volumes to me about how waiting patiently for the manifestation of God's supernatural love is worth the wait. It is far better than the instant gratification that comes with giving people a *"piece of my mind."*

Because I chose love over my *"right to retaliate,"* God blessed. Please note that I do not boast in myself but in the Holy Spirit who guides my natural man and has become my life's breath. He didn't bless me because of any personal greatness because I have none. He did bless it because He cannot help but bless His promise and that which comes only from Him. Choosing love in the face of hatred requires absolute faith that God's ways are always greater than our own. Love planted takes time to cultivate, but the fruit of God's labor will always bring a great harvest through our human vessel.

Within six weeks, she passed. I was honored to share in those remaining weeks by spending much quality time with her. She prayed with her nephew [a pastor] and made peace with God through that. In addition, she made peace with me after all those long, long years enduring much grief and heartache. This is an excellent testimony of why it is so important to follow God's rules. Not for the sake of Law, but for the sake of His love toward all mankind. We are to steer clear of quarrels and dissensions with anyone. It is a lesson for all people whether you're dealing with in-laws or other everyday life people. This is where the Word comes to life. Here are a few texts to remind us of how to properly conduct ourselves with all mankind:

> "Honor all people, love the brotherhood, fear God, honor the king (I Peter 2:17)."

> Now flee from youthful lusts and pursue righteousness, faith, love and peace, with those who call on Yahweh from a pure heart. But refuse foolish and ignorant speculations, knowing that they produce quarrels. Yahweh's bond-servant must not be quarrelsome, but be kind to all, able to teach, patient when wronged, with gentleness correcting those who are in opposition, if perhaps God may grant them repentance leading to the knowledge of the truth, and they may come to their senses and escape from the snare of the devil, having been held captive by him to do his will (II Timothy 2:22-26).

> "Know this, my beloved brothers: let every person be quick to hear, slow to speak, slow to anger (James 1:19)."

"Blessed are the peacemakers, for they shall be called sons of God (Matthew 5:9)."

"Bearing with one another and, if one has a complaint against another, forgiving each other; as Yahweh has forgiven you, so you also must forgive (Colossians 3:13)."

"Be angry and do not sin; do not let the sun go down on your anger…Let all bitterness and wrath and anger and clamor and slander be put away from you, along with all malice (Ephesians 4:26, 31)."

Learning from Mistakes:

When I look back over the last thirty-plus years and see all of the mistakes I made in both of my first two marriages, I have certainly learned from them. I did not know how to honor my in-laws as my own parents. However, the fantastic thing about our most holy God is that, once we learn better, He often allows us to correct our past misgivings.

In correlation to God's *"What's yours is mine"* marriage philosophy, it does away with the mindset that, should you divorce, you have exclusive dibs on whatever you brought into the marriage. It sounds harsh, but once we've entered the marriage covenant becoming *"one,"* all we possess before marriage is 100% and equally the spouses. There is no separation of property. If, by chance, both parties are willing to relinquish whatever the other brought to the table, that's one thing, but we can't rightfully get angry when they want to keep what we brought in. It's all common property.

Again, when we understand how God designed marriage to work, we will be much more cautious entering and much more cautious exiting. I cannot say it enough—let us seek the face and heart of our Creator to see who He has created for us. We will all better handle marital issues when we do. Only when His heart is front and center of every decision will things begin to work for good. Marriage will be smoother and more pleasurable. *"What's mine is mine, and what's theirs is theirs"* is a recipe for disaster. There is no separation of family or property.

Prayer:

Father, in the name of Jesus, show me the frailty of my own fleshly love so that I can come to You a broken vessel. As I commit my limited love to You, fill me with Your limitless, supernatural, abounding, abiding love. Reveal to me exactly how You have ordained marriage, that which is between my spouse and me, and also between my new family and me. Help me understand in my mind, heart, and spirit that they are as much my family as my spouse's, no matter how they treat me. Allow me to move, think, act, and speak according to Your Holy Spirit and never according to my fleshly man. I release myself and all of my frailty and failures to You, O God so that You are free to move through me according to Your way, will, plan and purpose. Expose to me every wicked way within me so that I can confess, repent, and be made whole in You. Give me eyes to see, ears to hear, and a mind to understand and comprehend Your heart, Jesus. For only in You can anything good come from this worthless, earthen vessel. You are the Potter, and I am the clay. Mold me, make me, and take me as You desire, O Lord. May I never shame you by conducting myself in a manner unworthy of Your Gospel. In Jesus' name, I pray and claim that I will walk according to the Spirit and not according to the flesh. Amen.

Notes

CHAPTER 25

How to Love Your Spouse

If you don't read any other chapter, this is the one to read! Here it is if you want to love as Christ loves His holy bride unconditionally. I am thankful to God every day for teaching me this because without this understanding, I was doomed to fail as a wife. Please know that this applies to men and women since God's love has no gender, no particular class or station, no political view, no race, and absolutely no prejudice. God's love is universal, and no one can mimic it. It must be us allowing His love, the genuine article, to flow through us.

Colossians 3 for Marriage:

> Therefore if you have been raised up with Christ, keep seeking the things above, where Christ is, seated at the right hand of God. Set your mind on the things above, not on the things that are on Earth. For you have died and your life is hidden with Christ in God. When Christ, who is our life, is revealed, then you also will be revealed with Him in glory. Therefore consider the members of your Earthly body as dead to immorality, impurity, passion, evil desire, and greed, which amounts to idolatry...now you also, put them *all* aside: anger, wrath, malice, slander, and abusive speech from your

mouth. Do not lie to one another, since you laid aside the old self with its evil practices…So, as those who have been chosen of God, holy and beloved, put on a heart of compassion, kindness, humility, gentleness and patience; bearing with one another, and forgiving each other, whoever has a complaint against anyone; just as Yahweh forgave you, so also should you. Beyond all these things put on love, which is the perfect bond of unity. Let the peace of Christ rule in your hearts, to which indeed you were called in *one body*; and be thankful. Let the word of Christ richly dwell within you (Colossians 3:1-9, 12-16).

The above text is an absolutely perfect description of how to treat our spouses. How many marriages end with one or both people exuding anger, wrath, malice, slander, abusive speech, and lying to one another. Notice the last line refers to being *"one body."* No one can escape this reality. I do realize this is about the body of Christ, but it can easily and aptly focus on marriage where *"two become one flesh."* The two people now residing together sharing the same food and space can readily grow out of love and into hatred if they don't keep their eye on the proverbial ball [supernatural, everlasting love of God] instead of the natural, limited, fleshly love.

It begins with urging us to seek continuously the things of Heaven, where Christ is. When we focus on the earthly stuff, we are doomed to failure. The earthly things within marriages are things that focus on self. When we limit our attention to selfish issues, big or small, we miss the bigger picture altogether. It also points out that we have *"died"* and are *"hidden in Christ."* This depicts our spiritual marriage to Christ—He is the groom, and we are His bride [singular as one *entity* in Him]. In marriage, when two become one, as repeated throughout, technically, both die, becoming one new creation. Again, something vital to consider before the *"I do's."*

When we see marriage as God sees it, we shan't be quite so hasty running to the altar. True love, the love of Christ, is sacrificial. Unless we recognize the true sacrifice required for a healthy marriage, even if we never divorce, the marriage is a falsehood, a pretense of sorts.

The Perfect Bond of Unity:

> Slaves, be obedient to those who are your masters according to the flesh, with fear and trembling, in the sincerity of your heart, as to Christ; not by way of eye service, as men-pleasers, but as slaves of Christ, doing God's will from the heart. With good will render service, as to Yahweh, and not to men, knowing that whatever good thing each one does, this he will receive back from Yahweh, whether slave or free (Ephesians 6:5-8).

Love is the perfect bond of unity. Marriage is a union. Without His love flowing through our veins, lips, and actions, how quickly the union will be split back into two pieces. To the chagrin of all who have experienced such a split, generally, we fragment into a million pieces laid bare on the ground waiting to be picked up by the garbage collector. Look at Ephesians 6 above.

Here we are again with the "*slave to master*" scenario. Where it refers to "*slaves,*" aren't we all slaves one to another? Previously, we defined "*bondservant*:" which we are called to be to God and one another. In marriage, since we know the husband and wife have each other, each is a "*slave,*" per se, to the other without bias. Again, it is a great point to ponder when deciding whom to marry. Always ask yourself, "*Would it be a problem being a slave to him or her the rest of my life?*" If the answer is, "*Yes, that would be a problem,*" you may want to seriously reconsider.

The point of both sets of text is to reiterate that, when we love, especially within a marital union, we are to love as "*unto God*" and

223

never as *"unto the person."* When we do love as unto the person, we will always be disappointed because of the flesh's imperfections. No matter how much in love we may be, no one will ever be able to fully satisfy us in any area. This is a life lesson I wish I had known before marrying the first and second time. It's a lesson I didn't learn and really comprehend until early into my third marriage. Once I got it, everything changed for the better.

If you recall the story about Michael's pornography and my poor reaction, we'll continue with this topic. Michael is generally a man of great integrity and loves me with all his heart. I knew this indiscretion was something about which he was neither flaunting nor happy. He wanted to change, but the pressure of the fear of losing his family only drove him to the very thing from which he was trying to refrain. Fear will always move us toward the thing we want to abandon. Since we have established that love covers a multitude of sins, the sooner we learn to love our spouses as Christ loves, honors, and respects the church [limitless grace and mercy], the better our marriages will be.

In addition to my transformation, Michael was also transformed. He has had no further issues with pornography. He confesses temptation, but he says temptation is further and further removed from him. The bottom line is that when we love as unto a person, we are always in a place of anticipation. We're always hoping, nay, expecting they will reciprocate our love in the way we extended love to them. The problem arises when they do not do so in like manner but in their own individual way. This leaves us disappointed continuously. By the fleshly nature, we constantly give love hoping to receive from them what we expect returned. This can never work and will always end in failure.

No one loves the same way. No one perceives precisely the same way how love should be manifested. For example, when I told him that I abhor pornography, I expected him to immediately stop just because I would do the same for him. But he isn't built the same way.

We all have different hang-ups and shortcomings, and no one can dictate how or when we change. In fact, it's inconsiderate as well as unreasonable to expect people to be a puppet on a string. Loving as unto the person keeps everyone in bondage.

On the other hand, sacrifice is never a problem when we see only God and love people as unto Him. We cease expecting the person to render back to us what we've given them, and we begin to rely on faith that God alone will generate perfect love for us. No longer is the other person expected to "*pay back*" what may never be in their "*love budget.*" The general population knows what it is to owe a financial debt we never have enough cash to pay—it's stifling. When we love expecting nothing in return, this is the love of Christ—selfless and sacrificial; loving despite their misdemeanors just as we appreciate the same love. When I changed and loved Michael exclusively as the Lord, Michael's debt was wiped clean, liberating us both. Loving as unto man is bondage. Loving as unto God extends His freedom.

Notes

CHAPTER 26

So Now What?

The most common response may leave one asking, "*So now what do I do?*" I've broken it into three categories.

Part I: Single and in a Wrong Relationship

If you are in a relationship not of God heading toward an unholy marital covenant, that's an easy one—end it and don't look back! Do not marry because you're thinking, "*We've come this far, so I can't back out now.*" It's simply not true. Before saying, "*I do,*" not after, is the best time to back out. However hard breaking up is before marriage, it is nothing compared to breaking up post-vows. You have not yet made a covenant vow.

Likewise, if you are in a relationship heading toward a holy covenant but engaging in sexual relations before marriage, stop, repent, receive forgiveness, and abstain until you are legal in the sight of God and man. When God's people wait upon right timing, the blessings abound far more abundantly than if you put the cart before the horse. If you are living together and the two of you are, in fact, ordained for one another, take the above measures and then proceed in proper timing.

After all, if it's an ordained relationship and you are *"burning,"* why wait to marry? Otherwise, we're back to stop sinning, repent, receive forgiveness, move out, and begin again in purity. There is no such thing as *"We're in too far, and we can't stop."* It's absolute rubbish! In Christ, anything is possible. Obedience to Yahweh may be difficult because you placed yourself in an inappropriate situation, but blessings always result from obedience, no matter how rigorous the realignment process.

Part II: Married and *You* Want a Divorce

If you are already married and miserable because you know you entered into marriage outside the will and direction of YHWH, it's a bit more complicated. If there are children involved, it's even more complex. Each person, or rather, each couple, must weigh everything very carefully. As previously mentioned, jumping out of marriage is not a fix-all to problems. Consequently, divorcing could very well cause increased problems and misery. Divorce should never be an option taken lightly.

One must consider all divorce effects, such as how it will impact the children, your spouse, your family, and you mentally and emotionally; the impact upon your finances, your home, and any future marriage that could result post-divorce. One must carefully ponder future ramifications as opposed to merely the here-and-now. Most importantly, each person must consider how it will strengthen or weaken their walk with God and testimony for or against Him.

I have encountered many marriages where divorce actually strengthened one or both people's walk because, while married, they exhausted all their energy on *"making"* things less miserable, but to no avail. *"Making"* is an act of force that is endlessly stressful; there was zero time to focus on the Kingdom of God—where our focus should remain. In these situations, the conclusion is to separate so that the individuals within the marriage can become whole again. Many times, though separated for many years, divorce never transpires. I must add, however, that if this is your situation, you do not have the God-leeway to engage in romantic relationships with other people, contrary to popular belief. If you have not legally divorced, you are married and must act accordingly.

In the case of abuse—physical, mental, emotional, sexual, I absolutely recommend leaving. If you and/or your children are in harm's way, how would remaining honor God? I know many ministers who have strongly advised abused wives to "*submit more*," and the end result was the wife's and/or children's death. This is tragic on levels I cannot express with mere words. Many ministers suggest, and even say outright, that if the woman is being abused, she is obviously doing something wrong. There are authorities in the land for such abuse, and the wife, or husband in some cases, should utilize the governing authority to the fullest extent. This does not mean unforgiveness should remain, but protection is vital.

In the case where two people have simply changed and grown apart over the years, this can be remedied if both the husband and wife are willing to meet in the middle and compromise [a dreaded word no one wants to hear]. Compromise does not mean one getts railroaded while the other gets everything they want. It does mean that both must willingly relinquish their selfish nature to produce the greater good for the Kingdom of God; this is recommended no matter the situation. Change must come from and for both the husband and wife.

"*Change*" is not a word that pleases people any more than "*compromise!*" Most people are dreadfully afraid of it and fight it with all their strength. Many would rather divorce than concede. It's viewed as a weakness when actually it's strength when led by Holy Spirit and not a people-pleasing spirit. Change, in this reference, does not mean "*making temporary changes just to appease or silence the spouse.*" It means conceding your current ways and taking a new nature and approach. This is a permanent transformation, not temporary. To reiterate, concession must come from *both*, or it will not work, or at least not very long.

Some may read this and say, "*I married the wrong person, and I secretly love the one I know I was supposed to marry. What do I do?*" Clearly, leaving one for the other is never a healthy choice, not ever. The focus should always be on the Kingdom of God and His righteousness. If, in this case, Christ is the focus and the marriage truly has no hope of survival, divorce may come. However, divorce should absolutely never be based on, "*As soon as I get a divorce, I'm going to marry the one I really love and should have married long ago.*" This is unhealthy and will only lead to further heartache, pain, and destruction because things were not handled correctly. When someone leaves to join someone else, disaster is imminent—you can bank on it.

Case I:

A good case is a very close friend who gave me permission to use her story. She did as described above; she would leave one bad marriage only when she knew someone else was waiting. She has been married and divorced four times. Three of the four husbands were abusive, and the other one was simply wrong. I did not know her then, but she described her actions as a result of looking for love in the wrong places and going about it entirely incorrectly. She even had an affair with a married minister.

Her father left her mother when she was little. Her mother spoiled her to compensate for the father's absence, yet inwardly resented her daughter for causing her husband to leave. All this left this little girl longing for some man, any man, to love her; never was she aware of the intense, boundless, irreversible love Yahweh already bestowed her. It also left her insecure that all men, and people in general, would leave her due to her perception of personal worthlessness.

At thirteen, she was already engaging in sex with her sixteen-year-old boyfriend, and he was physically abusing her. This began a long trail of bad relationships. She is now at peace with Yahweh and herself and realizes the destructive behavior of going from man to man. She recognizes that she conducted herself in this manner because of fear instead of faith in the Lord. Fear will always drive us right smack in the middle of the worst place. She finally dealt with her deeply seeded insecurities, and continues to realize that God is her Husband and Father. No one loves her as He. No one is worth jeopardizing her relationship with Jesus.

Until we allow God's restorative love to overtake us, we [men and women] will continuously hop from one bad relationship to another no matter how great it appears in the beginning. When people come to me for marital counseling, I always counsel them about the personal issues that lie within themselves and have been there since childhood. Until we deal with unresolved spiritual problems within ourselves, we can never fully be the spouse God intends whether we married the right or wrong person.

Case II:

I know a couple who married very young. The girl was pregnant as a teen, and the boy loved her deeply. Fast forward twenty years, and the husband started feeling restless. He still loves his wife and has not had an affair, but he thinks she has taken him for granted and does not correctly appreciate him. He feels trapped in their marriage because, deep down—or not so deeply, he wonders what he's missed in life. He wants to go places and experience things in which she has no interest. He is frustrated that he hasn't done more with his life and somehow justifies blaming her for getting pregnant at seventeen during their first sexual encounter.

Part of him wants to stay, and part wants to go. The "*go*" part romanticizes that things will be better, happier, and more exciting if divorced with a new start. Little does this man understand that he has not adequately considered their children, alimony; the hatred and bitterness that will mound, the financial strain it will further compound; the open shame, guilt, condemnation, and things of the like. Since they have children, he will always have to deal with her on some level; absolute separation would elude him. His *"fresh start"* will be stale before it's unwrapped! It wasn't long before he had an affair, nearly destroying their marriage and kids. Things were tumultuous, to say the least. Years later, they're still working through the betrayal to keep their marriage intact.

On the other hand, his wife feels like she has to completely change who she is for him to love her as he once did. She, too, feels resentment because she initially felt pressured by him to have sex when she wasn't sure. She was rough on him during their early years of marriage. Fast forward twenty years; now that he wants to leave, she's in love with him as he once was with her. She pleaded for him to stay with tears of desperation. The more she pleaded, the more disdain grew within him. This leads us to scenario number three.

Part III: Married and *Your Spouse* Wants a Divorce

The worst thing a person can do when their spouse wants to leave is begging, crying, pleading, and pleading some more. Of course, with the initial shock realizing they want to exit stage left, there will be anger and sorrow, probably mounted with tears and fears. However, once it settles a bit, no matter how much you feel the desire to beg and plead, resist. Let them go. We've all heard the old adage, *"If you love something, let it go. If it's true love, it'll come back to you."* It is too true. Certainly express love for them and convey your desire to remain and work on the marriage together, but this is not the same as begging.

If the one being left will allow the spouse the freedom to work through his or her issues, things will progress faster, healthier, and more productively. Just because you enable them to leave does not automatically mean divorce is imminent. Separation is just that—a time to be separate to clear one's head. Even if another person is involved, trying to force them to stay will only drive them away more quickly. It's very much like dealing with children. The more the parent insists they should not do something, the more they are drawn to it.

Let's face it, most adults are merely aged adolescents. People want what they want when they want it, and most will do anything necessary to obtain their wants. With the above couple, I can't blame the husband. After all, they were very young when they wed. There was initially no infidelity, just a time of feeling trapped and lost; many other factors weigh into the situation. People think and feel what they think and feel and must be allowed the leeway to work through it. The more people bury their feelings, the worse the explosion in the future. As in this case, it led to a physical affair.

Granted, I would highly recommend working through the issues as they develop instead of waiting years down the road, but too often, mounding and hidden feelings happen all too often, and one must be allowed to work through them. This is why godly counseling is always recommended. To the men reading this, please do yourself a favor and do not allow foolish pride to stand in the way of your potentially healthy marriage. Willingly seek a sound counselor and open yourself. To the women, I suggest not forcing the issue. The more you push, the more the men will shut down.

The worst thing one can do, as stated above, is to try changing everything about themselves to "*make*" the spouse love them. This is a bad idea any day of the week! Unless it is a genuine change led by Holy Spirit, it won't stick, and it will not make them love you more. In fact, more likely than not, your spouse will not gain but lose respect for you. You are who you are, not who you pretend to be. Only by working together to change collectively and changing the right things will change be productive. Merely working on the external is useless.

The aforementioned couple has a great chance of surviving and thriving if they would realize that nothing will ever be the same after talk of divorce and his affair. They will either get better, divorce, or remain married more miserable than ever—going back to status quo is not an option. It will be mandatory for both to meet in the middle, forgive each other of actual and perceived wrongs, and begin with a clean slate if they want to thrive. If either of them says or thinks something like, *"I can never forgive him or her for what was said or done,"* they are doomed to failure. Both must be able to recognize their own shortcomings and selfishness and seek Jesus for true alterations without using the *"But you did this and that"* card whenever they feel irritated.

The above scenario is more common for those who marry very young. The man hits a midlife crisis while the woman experiences insecurities of aging. Their youth caused them to act foolishly and selfishly, and, generally speaking, neither recognize it; therefore, their bad behavior toward one another never really changes. It merely shifts. No matter how they may mature in other areas, they still seem to treat one another in the childish ways of youth. In fact, until they hit a wall where divorce or separation is discussed, they usually don't recognize their own error. It requires something drastic for a wake-up call. When it comes, too many throw in the towel because there's too much work, change, and concessions that must be made. It appears easier to just start over as a single person. Again, this is foolhardy thinking.

I know another couple who divorced with two small children. In their situation, both cheated at different times. The husband who cheated first is now holding his ex-wife's adultery against her, threatening to expose all her indiscretions to their children just for vengeance's sake. Yet he's calling it righteousness because he's telling the *"truth;"* these are two professing followers of Christ. This is a prime example of a person so consumed with hatred and retaliation that he cannot and will not see the destruction he is causing his children, her, and himself. It is heartless and wicked behavior on even the best day. It is also a perfect example of just how far out of hand things get when, at first, divorce seems amicable. And just to be clear, an amicable divorce is a myth no matter how calm and kind people appear on the surface. Pain is always a result of divorce, no matter how necessary it may be.

This ex-wife is now having a sexual relationship with her new fiancé, and he is still married, though separated many years. This woman, mortified by her ex-husband's despicable behavior, equally acts outside God's will. The old expression *"the pot calling the kettle black"* would aptly apply. She reasons her behavior is not hurtful to anyone. She also sat in judgment against a family member years prior because of the appearance of fornication. She told her children, *"So and so is an adulterer"* and defined *"adultery"* to them. Make no mistake, God is not mocked; as you judge, you will do; whatever you sow, you will eventually reap (Galatians 6:7). Whenever we wonder how our lives became such a mess, we might first need to look in the spiritual mirror and assess how we have treated others in judgment, bitterness, and spiritual snobbery.

In any given divorce scenario, no matter the cause, it is imperative to have a period of healing, a time of pulling back to gather your thoughts, seek God's heart, and regroup. When one immediately remarries, the season of healing is not allowed because of the rush. In this, the wounds transfer from one marriage to the next, and things such as guilt, condemnation, fear, sorrow, anger, etc., will begin to fester and spread like a plague. Even if they think they will never experience this because of their true love—of God or not, they are entirely mistaken. God would never condone such bad behavior; therefore, we should never deceive ourselves into believing that God could somehow bless our mess. As I've written throughout this book, obedience to God's heart leads where He knows best, whatever that best is.

Part IV: Neither Wants a Divorce, but It is Necessary:

My friend and first ex-husband's second ex-wife, Melissa, finalized her divorce after his countless affairs and indiscretions. Within five months post-divorce, she remarried an old acquaintance. Against

235

everyone's better judgment, she married anyway. I started counseling her as soon as she sent our ex packing. I told her all the reasons why she should refrain from any romantic relationships until her soul wounds were healed properly. Regardless, she married.

Unfortunately for her, this husband nearly beat the life out of her. Every time she would leave him, he would beg her to return because she was *"his one true love."* Reasonably, she did not want to be a three-time-divorcee. Her first husband cheated, her second husband cheated, and her third husband was violent and cheated. The second husband was a sociopath, and the third was a psychopath. In her case, so to save her life, divorce was mandatory. She kept going back, kept getting the daylights beaten out of her, and finally she cut the cord and is now divorced. He insisted he didn't want a divorce, but he was a most unhealthy person. She didn't want a divorce, but wanted to remain alive on Earth a while longer.

I could go on and on about this situation, but for sake of moving on, I'll leave it right here. Sometimes, though neither may want a divorce, it saves lives.

Notes

CHAPTER 27

Unbreakable Marriage, part I

Part I: Before Marriage

"Abstain from the appearance of evil (I Thessalonians 5:22)."

But take care that this liberty of yours does not somehow become a stumbling block to the weak. For if someone sees you, who has knowledge, dining in an idol's temple, will not his conscience, if he is weak, be strengthened to eat things sacrificed to idols? For through your knowledge he who is weak is ruined, the brother for whose sake Christ died. And so, by sinning against the brethren and wounding their conscience when it is weak, you sin against Christ. Therefore, if food causes my brother to stumble, I will never eat meat again, so that I will not cause my brother to stumble (I Corinthians 8:9-13).

In chapter fifteen's first paragraph, "*Why Choose Purity*," in my book, *Discovering the Person of Holy Spirit*, volume II, I wrote:

Our Heavenly Father is so very serious about abstaining from evil and being pure that He states in I Thessalonians 5:22, "*Abstain from all appearance of evil.*" Purity is crucial for every believer. This is not solely for you as an individual, but for those who may be caused to stumble from the impression of sin. For instance, if you have a boyfriend or girlfriend and you are abstaining from a sexual relationship until marriage but you choose to spend the night with one another, even though God knows what you are not doing, it has the potential to be evil to the spiritually weak. This is because the world around you [neighbors, family, onlookers] do not know what isn't going on. If it appears to be sin and it makes another stumble, it becomes sin. Perception is the onlooker's reality, even if their perception is incorrect. (end excerpt)

Men and women seeking all of God's very best for their marriages pursue righteousness with a steadfast mission. They seek cleanliness before God in all of their ways, especially in the area of sexual purity. Many professing Christians lean much more toward looking for a spiritual loophole rather than seeking obedience to the greatest degree. They reason, "*Well, I answer to God and God alone. I know what I am and am not doing. I don't have to answer to man.*"

Immediately, I refer to I Corinthians 8. The words "*idol's temple*" in modern-day can be any place—literal or metaphorical—where an onlooker could easily understand that we, the ones with knowledge of God's Word, are sinning against the very God we proclaim outwardly to love and obey. Why would we or anyone who loves Yahweh do anything that could even remotely give the spiritually weak or immature a reason to sin? Indeed, it is a selfish person who thinks only of him or herself over the needs of others. Most of what people do is for the good of self disguised as being for the greater good of God's Kingdom.

I constantly hear, "*We're moving in together before marriage for financial reasons. We aren't doing anything wrong, so my conscience is clear. We can tithe and give offerings more if we consolidate our finances as soon as possible."* They claim their reasons are for *"tithes and offerings,"* yet it's really because that's what they want and choose to do. Where is the integrity of God's people? We can rationalize anything and then turn and expect God to bless our poor decisions. II Peter 3:16 (The Message Bible), reads, *"Some things Paul writes are difficult to understand with people of this mindset. Irresponsible people who don't know what they are talking about twist them every way. They do it to the rest of the Scriptures, too, destroying themselves as they do it."*

There are many reasons why men and women cannot live together before marriage. The first of which, no matter how good a couple's intentions may be, the flesh always gets in the way. Hormones run wild. Passion peaks. They eventually engage in non-sex, as if that exists, which is sexual misconduct without the act of intercourse. Any sexual activity between a man and a woman is fornication lest they are married. Few, if any, can genuinely be pure while cohabitating pre-nuptials. It's difficult enough just dating and living separately.

Also, living together as man and wife is set aside expressly for marriage, not for the engaged, aka not married. Nowhere do we see people of the Bible establishing a household before the marriage giving it a *"trial run"* or to *"test the goods,"* as many so crudely say. Marriage is based on trust. More specifically, trusting God that, when the time is right, living together will work because God is blessing what He ordained. Most people who live together before marriage either never get around to the marriage because they become complacent or they're under the misconception that things will be no different once married; those people are greatly deceived. They have a false perception of single people living together and married people living together—it is altogether different. Living together outside the marriage covenant is not the same as within.

Engaged couples must think of why it is against God to live together before marriage rather than why it is *"okay."* Living together before marriage sets a false standard and gives the impression of fornication whether it is happening or not. Why would anyone genuinely more concerned for the perfect will of God do anything to jeopardize the full blessings He has in store? I ask this question a lot because I see so much where people simply do not think of the ramifications of their poor decisions. The real question is, *"Where is your heart?"* Is it set on God or fleshly, instant gratification? None of His instruction is about following the Law, for Christ fulfilled the Law. However, following His commands is about understanding that He set them in place for our good. When we truly believe His laws are of Love and not bondage, it will change our perspective on everything.

"The faith which you have, have as your own conviction before God. Happy is he who does not condemn himself in what he approves. But he who doubts is condemned if he eats because his eating is not from faith, and whatever is not from faith is sin," states Romans 14:22-23. It is imperative in any decision-making to be sure the decisions are based on faith in God and faith-based on God's Word. We need to make certain that we do not condemn ourselves by what we approve. Always ask yourself, *"If I had to stand before God right now to give an answer for this decision, would I make the same one?"* If we genuinely seek God's will, always check the God-gage. What we approve in this life, be it marriage or anything else, make certain it meets God's approval lest we begin to doubt and find ourselves in something not so easily remedied. My eighth-grade rule of thumb is *"when in doubt, do without."*

I remember someone asking me years ago, *"What's the big deal about marriage? How much can things really change? We're in love now; we'll be in love later."* It isn't enough to build a lasting marriage no matter how much *"in love"* you are or think you are. Human love [based on emotion] comes and goes, but it is not necessarily the true love of God. Things such as politics, religion, finances, jobs, where to live—house, city, state or country, children—birth, death, health, how to raise them, whether you want them, can or will have them, how they act, merging them from previous marriages, and more, parents—interference with your marriage, their death or illness, if they should live with you, near you, by themselves, or in a home for the elderly, career goals, fundamental interests, affairs—of the heart, body, or mind, and a plethora of other issues can change everything. Unless your marital commitment is unto God instead of the person, there is little chance the marriage will thrive. Marital success is not how long a couple stays together, but the quality of everyday life lived for Christ. Since marriage was created by God, marriage can be successful only when ordained by Him and following His ways.

If you can't see yourself totally submitting to your fiancé—male or female, they are not for you. If you can't imagine your fiancé gaining significant weight, developing a long-term illness, or care for them if they are paraplegic or anything of the like, they are not for you. If you can't see yourself still in love with your fiancé for any reason, they are not for you. My rule of thumb, along with God's voice and His direction, is to imagine your *"worst-case scenario."* If you cannot see yourself remaining in the marriage in that scenario, they are not for you. One never knows what the future holds.

Part II: Undefiled Marriage Bed

> "Marriage is to be held in honor among all, and the marriage bed is to be undefiled; for fornicators and adulterers God will judge (Hebrews 13:4)."

First, let's look at Samson and Delilah from Judges 16, one of the Bible's most unholy couples. I will explain what is wrong and why. Then we can move on to how to embark upon a holy, unbreakable union.

> Now Samson went to Gaza and saw a *harlot* there, and went in to her...after this it came about that he loved a woman in the valley of Sorek, whose name was Delilah. The lords

of the Philistines came up to her and said to her, «Entice him, and see where his great strength lies and how we may overpower him that we may bind him to afflict him. Then we will each give you eleven hundred pieces of silver.» So Delilah said to Samson, «Please tell me where your great strength is and how you may be bound to afflict you…Then Delilah said to Samson, "Behold, you have deceived me and told me lies; now please tell me how you may be bound…up to now you have deceived me and told me lies; tell me how you may be bound… How can you say, 'I love you,' when your heart is not with me? You have deceived me these three times and have not told me where your great strength is." It came about when she pressed him daily with her words and urged him, that his soul was annoyed to death. So he told her all that was in his heart…When Delilah saw that he had told her all that was in his heart, she sent and called the lords of the Philistines, saying, "Come up once more, for he has told me all that is in his heart." Then the lords of the Philistines came up to her and brought the money in their hands. She made him sleep on her knees, and called for a man and had him shave off the seven locks of his hair. Then she began to afflict him, and his strength left him. She said, "The Philistines are upon you, Samson!" And he awoke from his sleep and said, "I will go out as at other times and shake myself free." But he did not know that Yahweh had departed from him. Then the Philistines seized him and gouged out his eyes; and they brought him down to Gaza and bound him with bronze chains, and he was a grinder in the prison… Thus he had judged Israel twenty years (Judges 16:1, 4-6, 11, 13, 15-21, 31).

We first see Samson drawn to a harlot. This is the first clue he was not a man who utilized the wisdom God gave him. Instead, he was led by feelings, emotions, and sight [that to which his fleshly man was drawn instead of the Spirit of God]. Delilah was from Sorek. It is not clear exactly where this valley of Sorek was located, but we know it was a valley separating the Land of Judah from the Philistines. Sorek is often known as a *"fruitless tree"* or *"empty"* in Hebrew. However, another etymology suggests that *"sorek"* means *"special vine"* and refers to the grapes and wines grown in the area. Basically, we can see Sorek as *"middle ground,"* the proverbial fence that Christ-followers so often straddle, leading us to fruitlessness.

He had no business in Sorek, much less to fall in love with one of their women. It does not say whether or not Samson married Delilah, and more than likely, he did not. As a result, chaos ensued. We all know this story, so there's no need to lay it out in its entirety. I do want to point out how harmful, even deadly, an unholy union is in Christ's sight and in our earthly tents. He may have loved her, but she did not love him. She quickly sold out to Samson's enemy. It's always startling to me what so many will do for a few dollars.

I find it interesting that Samson ruled for twenty years yet left this life too early because of the love of one ungodly woman. Pride caused Samson to continuously allow her to tempt him. He had all strength and power from the anointing of Almighty God just as Solomon had wisdom. Despite this touch of God, he gave himself over to a wicked woman, Delilah. Twice she tricked him, though both times, he toyed with her as if it were a game. When he realized she had deceived him, why didn't he leave her? Why did he allow her to continue in her apparent quest to destroy him? When it happened a third time, he told her the truth from her persistent pressure. We know the third time is when he was overtaken by the Philistines. Why would he toy with such a deceitful woman? A wicked soul tie was so strong that he willingly gave himself to her instead of separating. Anyone with eyes can see there had to be something more profound than the flesh compelling him to be so foolish.

Notes

CHAPTER 28

Unbreakable Marriage, part II

Adam and Eve:

Let's back up once again to Adam and Eve. They are the most famous couple in existence. Adam was alone in the garden.

> Then Yahweh God said, "It is not good for the man to be alone; I will make him a helper suitable for him."…So Yahweh God caused a deep sleep to fall upon the man, and he slept; then He took one of his ribs and closed up the flesh at that place. Yahweh God fashioned into a woman the rib which He had taken from the man, and brought her to the man. The man said, "This is now bone of my bones, and flesh of my flesh; she shall be called Woman, because she was taken out of Man." For this reason a man shall leave his father and his mother, and be joined to his wife; and they shall become one flesh. And the man and his wife were both naked and were not ashamed (Genesis 2:18, 21-25).

This couple was ordained of God creating the woman for the man. She was to be a helper. Since this ordained marital union, we have made a tragedy of what God set in motion for good. Women are not to seek a husband. The man should be watching for the one God created specifically for him while seeking God's Kingdom and acting accordingly. All of us, men and women, are to seek God's Kingdom above all else—I'm pretty sure I've driven that point home. When our eyes are on God, we will make holy, godly decisions, including those concerning marriage and holy relationships.

When we see marriages between two ordained in marriage in the Bible, we see holiness, wholeness, and purity. E.g., Ruth and Boaz, Zachariah and Elizabeth, Mary and Joseph, Abraham and Sarah, Pricilla and Aquilla, and even Gomer and Hosea. These couples, and many more, usheced God's will. By no means were they perfect. By no means were their marriages without issues, but, in their obedience to Yahweh, they did work through whatever was set before them. We know that whoever has a heart set on God's plan, their problems are merely catalysts for going higher in Christ.

To properly build an unbreakable marriage, we must first look at what God considers holy conduct overall, not exclusively within marriage. We need to see how to conduct ourselves in a holy manner before marriage to lay a solid foundation for the union. We need to learn as early as possible what covenant is and how to walk in and maintain it whether it is covenant with God, business, marriage, or other. Here are a few final thoughts to summarize the book This leaves much for all to ponder:

1. *"He who finds a wife finds a good thing and obtains favor from Yahweh* (Proverbs 18:22)." The word *"wife"* does not mean any woman just because the man married. This wife understands the fear of the Lord, a woman who does not become a nag, full of control and manipulation. Proverbs 21:9 says, *"It is better to dwell in a corner of the housetop than with a brawling* [nagging] *woman in a wide house."* I think that's clear enough!

2. *"Do not give your strength to women, or your ways to that which destroys kings...charm is deceitful, and beauty is vain, but a woman who fears YHWH, she shall be praised* (Proverbs 31:3, 30)." A man who foolishly gives himself over to a woman whose beauty is merely outward is a fool. Men, the Lord cautions you to be wise, to seek a woman who loves Him above all else. That does not infer *"any woman who loves God,"* but it's a direction leading to the holy one for you specifically. Men, you, too, need to have the fear of Yeshua before ever considering marriage.

3. *"No one can serve two masters; for either he will hate the one and love the other, or he will be devoted to one and despise the other. You cannot serve God and wealth* (Matthew 6:24)." If God is not truly your Master before marriage, you will unwittingly find yourself in a situation where you will, over time, have to choose between God and your spouse. *"Wealth"* is not just money, but that which you cherish. This is why we are not to be unequally yoked (II Corinthians 6:14). When two people are unequally yoked, it causes division with God and the marriage.

4. All of this is why Paul instructs in I Corinthians 7:8-9, *"But I say to the unmarried and to widows that it is good for them if they remain even as I. But if they do not have self-control, let them marry, for it is better to marry than to burn with passion."* It is wise to watch your company. We all know that bad company corrupts good character (I Corinthians 15:33). If you position yourself to limit your company to those who would not cause you to have to choose between obedience to the Master and those who could easily master you, you leave no foothold open to the enemy (Ephesians 4:27).

5. Finally, Proverbs 8:35-36 reads, *"For he who finds me [wisdom] finds life and obtains favor from Yahweh. But he who sins against me [wisdom] injures himself; all those who hate me [wisdom] love death."* This word is to men and women, young and old. Seek wisdom from God, not of the world. There is a difference.

6. "But the wisdom that is from above is first pure, then peaceable, gentle, and easy to be entreated, full of mercy and good fruits, without partiality, and without hypocrisy" is written in James 3:17 (KJV). Anyone who desires wisdom from God shall indeed have it. When you operate in it, you will know the voice of the Good Shepherd. When you know His voice and adhere to it, your steps will not slip.

Part III: Sacrificial Love (continued from chapter 27)

"An argument started among them as to which of them might be the greatest…the one who is least among all of you, this is the one who is great (Luke 9:46, 48)."

Then He poured water into the basin, and began to wash the disciples' feet and to wipe them with the towel with which He was girded…Jesus answered and said to him, "What I do you do not realize now, but you will understand hereafter"… You call Me Teacher and Lord; and you are right, for so I am. If I then, the Lord and the Teacher, washed your feet, you also ought to wash one another's feet. For I gave you an example that you also should do as I did to you. Truly, truly, I say to you, a slave is not greater than his master, nor is one who is sent greater than the one who sent him. If you know these things, you are blessed if you do them (John 13:5, 7, 13-17).

...be subject to one another in the fear of Christ. Wives, be subject to your own husbands, as to the Lord. For the husband is the head of the wife, as Christ also is the head of the church, He Himself being the Savior of the body. But as the church is subject to Christ, so also the wives ought to be to their husbands in everything. Husbands, love your wives, just as Christ also loved the church and gave Himself up for her (Ephesians 5:21-25).

Above everything written here, I pray everyone adheres to the crucial element of humility. The man should willingly submit to his wife in love, and, likewise, the woman should willingly submit to her husband in love. Humility is love. Love is humility. If Jesus Himself, the Teacher and Lord, would stoop lowly to wash the feet of His disciples—not excluding Judas, the one He already knew would betray Him, who are any of us to refuse humbling ourselves? Who are any of us to deny our spouse that which is otherwise something we would rather not do. Of course, it should go without saying that I am not speaking of anything outside God's will. If your spouse requests something unholy of you, God is your higher authority, and you should follow God's way instead of man—or woman.

Imagine a world where both husband and wife would set themselves aside placing the needs of their spouse above their own. Neither spouse should be as the disciples when they foolishly asked Jesus, *"Who is the greatest among us?"* Obviously, they were speaking from their flesh and not from the Spirit of God. No one can conduct themselves within the parameters of true sacrificial love if they are thinking with their selfish flesh.

When I hear couples say, *"Well, I won't do thus and so for him or her because they won't do thus and so for me,"* I can't help but cringe a bit internally. We should willingly be so committed to the covenant between ourselves and our spouse that nothing *we* do is motivated by what they do. The worst action we can take in this life is based on what others do or say. If the individuals within the marriage have such a poor attitude, no wonder marriages are falling apart at the seams! Jesus says, "*If you know these things, you are blessed if you do them.*" If you desire to be blessed, follow the direction of our Most High God; humble yourself, put your spouse above yourself, and lend service even to those you know have or will betray you. It's a lot to process, but again, we would have far fewer marriages if we thought of this before marriage. Blessings to each of you in whatever state you are!

Prayer:

Father, I pray with all my being that You reveal to me what is holy in Your sight. I thank You, because of Your Holy Spirit who dwells within me, that You have already given me wisdom from on high; You have readily supplied me with everything required to walk in self-discipline and holiness. Grant me the wisdom to utilize to the fullest extent the power of Holy Spirit instead of my flesh. May I be wise in all of my decisions about relationships, engagements, marriage, divorce, and everything concerning my future hope in You. I desire to marry only the one You designed for me and only me. I want to work through every life issue with my spouse as one entity instead of attempting to stand as two individuals. Show me how to respect, love, and honor my spouse as You love and honor Your holy bride. May I put You above all else, and then my spouse above myself. Knit our hearts together as one as You intend us to be. Allow me the privilege to view marriage as You know it is and not as I wish it were. I choose today to honor You in spirit, soul, mind, and body, whatever that sacrifice requires. I love You, O Lord, above all else. Direct my steps. Selah.

**If you do not know Christ, please read the *"Introduction to Christ"* section after the index.

Notes

Basic Marital Tips

1. Always speak truth in love. Fibbing, fabricating, embellishing, sugar coating, and anything of the kind should not happen. Lies will always catch up to you even if they seem otherwise microscopic and insignificant. Once you appear a liar, it takes a very long time to overcome. Have enough trust and respect for one another to be honest. In the end, it will serve well within your marriage. It's better to hear a painful truth than a beautiful lie.

2. Healthy communication is the key to any successful relationship, marriage or other. Do not hit the heart. Keep all arguments from the neck up.

3. As humorous this may sound, do your best to not go in the bathroom with your spouse. Silly, possibly, but when you see "*too much*," it can eventually dampen the romantic and sexual spark. This has to do with respecting personal privacy. Your spouse may fear expressing their need for privacy.

4. Always look for your spouse's positive aspects and compliment them. This is both encouraging as well as a reminder that you love, respect, and honor them.

5. Always touch. Not everything has to be sexual, but everything must originate from love and the impression of intimacy. A caress as you walk through a room will suffice. Hand holding or linking arm-in-arm is a small gesture to remind your spouse you are still attracted to them.

6. Take time from your busy day to sacrifice something on their behalf. Go somewhere with them you otherwise would not go.

7. Be generous. *"Generous"* can cover a broad spectrum, so discover what generosity means to your spouse and then extend their version of generosity. It goes back to, *"Do unto others as you would have them do unto you"* versus *"do for them what you would like yourself."* In other words, *"as you would have them do unto you"* means to love them the way they like to be loved, not how you like to be loved.

8. Be considerate. Always consider their needs and desires in addition to your own. E.g. if you lean toward harsher language but your spouse finds it inconsiderate, refrain, at least while you are in their company. Although we all know that such language should be eradicated, no one is perfect. Be thoughtful.

9. Never insult your spouse in the presence of others. Likewise, do not have what should be a private discussion in public to humiliate them. In private or in public, do not humiliate your spouse. Always purpose to have healthy discussions about your disagreements. Insults should be off the table.

10. When your spouse has a different opinion, don't take it personally as though it's a slight against you. Always allow them the freedom to agree to disagree without starting a fight or pouting.

11. Don't be insecure and self-abasing. There are few things less appealing or less attractive than self-loathing.

12. Be confident in your Christ-identity so you don't allow your husband or wife's identity to overshadow you. Knowing who you are allows you to embrace who they are without rivalry.

13. Always purpose to build your spouse, never tear them down. Love does not destroy, it encourages.

14. Before speaking or acting in anger, pause. Think about the possible repercussions of saying negative words or doing something hurtful. Consider a better way to express your feelings.

15. If you want your marriage to heal, first seek your own healing.

16. Never try to "*fix*" your spouse. Love them unconditionally. Speak to them in a way to which you would like to be spoken.

17. Do not badmouth your spouse to others if you genuinely want your marriage to remain or become healthy. Speak kindly or not at all. Seeking spiritually mature counsel is good, but keep in mind that most outside voices lack such mature wisdom.

18. Do not poke the bear, in a manner of speaking! If you know his or her tics and irritants, do not purposely do those things as though it's funny.

19. Do not take your spouse for granted. This should be an easy one, but all too often, it happens unawares.

20. Engage. Open yourself to your spouse. Willingly bare your heart without fear of what they'll think.

21. Listen. Hear what your spouse has to say without judgment or trying to remedy their problems. More often than not, just listening is sufficient.

22. Be aware. Pay close attention to the little details. Notice when your husband or wife is in need without them saying a word.

23. Pray with your spouse. If they aren't open to that, pray for them. There's power in prayer. God can do far more than you!

24. Do not badger, harass, or nag as it is a total turnoff and will push them away.

25. Do not beg. You are not a slave to your spouse. Ask politely but do not beg like a stray dog.

26. Do not abuse. Obviously, do not physically harm your spouse. Beyond that, do not threaten to take something away if they won't comply. Do not threaten because that is mental and emotional abuse.

27. Do not bribe. Love is giving and should not require an *"if you do this, I'll do that"* atmosphere. You and your spouse are one person and must act accordingly.

28. Keep your word. The best rule of thumb is to not quickly make a promise you aren't 100% sure you can keep. This will minimize you losing credibility.

29. Don't be jealous, paranoid, or accusatory as they are counterproductive. These characteristics are a negative, not a positive, and will eventually push away the one you're trying so hard to keep close.

30. Love, love, and love some more! Love covers a multitude of sin.

Index

Introduction to Christ

If you have come across this book, and you have never been properly introduced to God, this closing is a brief overview of how to come into the Kingdom of God.

Believe:

> "He then brought them out and asked, 'Sir, what must I do to be saved?' They replied, *'Believe in the Lord Jesus*, and you will be saved (Acts 16:29).'"

> "For John came to you to show you the way of righteousness, and you did not believe him, but the tax collectors and the prostitutes did. And even after you saw this, you did not repent and believe him (Matthew 21:32)."

"For all have sinned and fall short of the glory of God" is found in Romans 3:23. You must believe that you dwell in a sinful nature derived from Adam and The Fall of mankind. Secondly, you must believe that Jesus is Lord, that He gave His life for sinful mankind [you], and accept His supernatural gift. It is simultaneously the easiest and hardest decision of anyone's life.

In response to such a belief in the Savior, you can take hold of this Scripture, *"Whosoever shall call on the name of the Lord shall be saved,"* in Acts 2:21." You are *"whosoever."* Call out to Him—He's waiting.

Repentance Requirement:

"This is what is written: The Messiah will suffer and rise from the dead on the third day, and *repentance for the forgiveness of sins* will be preached in His name to all nations…(Luke 24:46-47).»

"Jesus answered them, 'It is not the healthy who need a doctor, but the sick. I have not come to call the righteous, but *sinners to repentance* (Luke 5:31-32).»

Repentance is a turning and returning. It is turning away [turning your back] from one direction to another, and then turning toward God. It's an act of absolute humility, which is also a requirement for God's presence to rest upon you. Repentance ushers God's grace through humility.

Baptism to Eternal Life:

"For *you have died* and your life is hidden with Christ in God (Colossians 3:3).»

"I baptize you with water, but He will *baptize you with the Holy Spirit* (Mark 1:8).»

"He who has believed and has been *baptized shall be saved*; but he who has disbelieved shall be condemned (Mark 16:16)."

"Therefore we have been *buried with Him through baptism into death*, so that as Christ was raised from the dead through the glory of the Father, so we too might walk in newness of life (Romans 6:4)."

"For all of you who were baptized into Christ have clothed yourselves with Christ (Galatians 3:27)."

Baptism takes belief a step further. Baptism, contrary to the modern-day church, *precedes* salvation not *succeeds*. This is not physical baptism, but spiritual. We are to surrender ourselves unto death in the spiritual sense to be able to receive a spiritual new life; hence the Galatians 2:20, "*I have been crucified in Christ; therefore it's no longer I who live but Christ who lives in me.*"

Baptism, metaphorically speaking, is the equivalent of crucifixion, aka death to self. We are "*buried in His death.*" When we come to Christ, we must see ourselves as dead so that we can receive His life. Just praying a "*sinner's prayer*"—which isn't scriptural—is not the same as surrender. Surrender is death.

Think about it like this. When one drowns, it's because they can no longer breathe underwater. If they could, they'd save their own life. When they finally recognize they have no power to rescue themselves, they literally surrender their lives unto a watery death. When we take on Christ's baptism [water of the Word], we must visualize ourselves as "*going under.*" We are drowning our natural man because we have no power to save ourselves. In the spirit-realm, we baptize into death all that came from Adam's bloodline. In this death condition, we are now available to take His new life. We are regenerated by a new bloodline from Jesus of heaven. We take a brand new origin. We are no longer "*of the earth*" but are "*of heaven.*" This is how we become "*strangers in the land of earth.*"

With this new origin, we must think from the vantage of our homeland, which is the Kingdom of God. This level of surrender causes a person to stop giving in to natural temptations, which brings us back to understanding we have but one nature while occupying space in another nature. You are not your flesh or any of its feelings, desires, or temptations. When tempted with sexual sin [homosexuality, adultery, pornography, pedophilia, or fornication, bestiality], in any form, the flesh wants what it wants, no doubt. However, the surrendered spirit [the real you] within a human shell desires to please the One who gave him a new eternal life. In this condition, he will say *"No"* emphatically because he comprehends that life in the flesh is nothing short of despair, anguish, suffering, and destruction.

Drowning in Christ causes the newness. You cannot have newness without first *"drowning."* Many in the modern-day church preach. *"Accept Christ and then be baptized with water immersion."* However, Scriptures would indicate the opposite. We are to believe in the Father and Son unto salvation, be baptized into His Spirit, then water baptism may follow. The man on the cross received the Kingdom of heaven through faith, yet was never water baptized. Unfortunately, we often misrepresent the purpose of baptism as if it's merely by water, or a prerequisite to receive God's Kingdom.

Grace and Repentance:

"Produce fruit in keeping with repentance (Matthew 3:8)."

"Three times I pleaded with the Lord to take it away from me. But He said to me, 'My grace is sufficient for you, for my power is made perfect in weakness.' Therefore I will all the more gladly boast about my weaknesses, so that Christ's power may rest on me (II Corinthians 12:8-9,)."

"For it is by grace you have been saved, through faith – and this is not from yourselves, it is the gift of God, not by works, so that no one can boast (Ephesians 2:8-9)."

Definition of Grace:

1. the free and unmerited favor of God, as manifested in the salvation of sinners and the bestowal of blessings
2. God giving you what you do not deserve (heaven vs. hell; life vs. death; peace vs. chaos)
3. the catalyst for an otherwise impossible transformation from the old man of Adam to the new man in Christ

Definition of Repentance:

1. to turn from sin and dedicate oneself to the amendment of one's life
2. to feel regret or contrition *leading* to change one›s mind
3. to cause to feel regret or contrition
4. to feel sorrow, regret, or contrition

Anyone teaching grace outside repentance and surrender is a false teacher. Surrender and repentance are required to receive God's grace. Yes, we live in the Day of Grace, so it is extended to all mankind on a general level, but in respect to walking in personal grace regularly comes through a heart rent before a Holy God. In this condition of perpetual repentance of the sin-nature, His grace is surely sufficient for you and whatever situational crisis you may face.

When I write "*perpetual repentance*," I mean walking continually in an attitude of cosigning all the lusts of the flesh unto God. It's as the Scripture directs, "*Being ready to punish all disobedience until personal obedience is achieved.*" An attitude of repentance does not mean "*self-abase*" because that is sin (Colossians 2:18, 23). Insulting, belittling, and beating oneself is self-abasement—that is not repentance. Repentance insists that you apologize to God for your action(s), go and sin no more, and continue unashamedly going about the Father's business. In true repentance, you are neither ashamed nor boastful in yourself because self is dead to the world and its lusts. Fruit of the Spirit of God can manifest only from a place of humility leading to repentance, which leads to grace.

Faith:

> "Now faith is confidence in what we hope for and assurance about what we do not see. This is what the ancients were commended for (Hebrews 11:1-2)."

> "Without faith it is impossible to please God (Hebrews 11:6)."

> "Therefore, since we have been justified by faith, we have peace with God through our Lord Jesus Christ, through whom we have gained access by faith into this grace in which we now stand. And we boast in the hope of the glory of God (Romans 5:1-2)."

Faith is an extension of belief, but stronger than belief alone. Even the demons believe and shudder (James 2:19). Faith says, "*I not only believe You exist, but I place all my hope in You,*" unlike the demons. Faith moves the immovable, touches the untouchable, and makes the impossible possible.

Forgiveness:

> "Therefore, my friends, I want you to know that through Jesus, the forgiveness of sins is proclaimed to you. Through Him, everyone who believes is set free from every sin, a justification you were not able to obtain under the law of Moses (Acts 13:38-39)."

Forgiveness has been extended by God through Jesus to all mankind, whether or not any of us receive it. It was granted to all mankind at the cross and resurrection of Christ. To receive it, all you must do is repent and it's yours. From there, the rest will come with great ease!

Repent to God. Accept His forgiveness. Forgive others. Let go of the shame, guilt, remorse, and condemnation. Let go of the lies, fear, doubt, and anxiety that lead you further and further into darkness.

A New Master!

"For sin shall no longer be your master, because you are not under the law, but under grace (Romans 6:14)."

"If the Son sets you free, you will be free indeed (John 8:36)."

"But now that you have been *set free from sin* and have become *slaves of God*, the benefit you reap leads to holiness, and the result is eternal life (Romans 6:22)."

"It is for freedom that Christ has set us free. Stand firm, then, and do not let yourselves be burdened again by a yoke of slavery (Galatians 5:1)."

"' I have the right to do anything,' you say – but not everything is beneficial. 'I have the right to do anything' – but I will not be mastered by anything (I Corinthians 6:12)."

"In him and through faith in him we may approach God with freedom and confidence (Ephesians 3:12)."

"You, my brothers and sisters, were called to be free. But do not use your freedom to indulge the flesh; rather, serve one another humbly in love. For the entire law is fulfilled in keeping this one command: 'Love your neighbor as yourself (Galatians 5:13-14).'"

Once you were alienated from God and were enemies in your minds because of your evil behavior. But now He has reconciled you by Christ's physical body through death to present you holy in His sight, without blemish and free from accusation – if you continue in your faith, established and firm, and do not move from the hope held out in the gospel. This is the gospel that you heard and that has been proclaimed to every creature under heaven, and of which I, Paul, have become a servant (Colossians 1:21-23)."

There is no greater gift from God than freedom! There is no greater pleasure or fulfillment in life than serving such a master because this Master is like no other. He is Father, Husband, Comforter, Healer, Redeemer, Forgiver. This is a master I can follow through eternity!

By surrendering to such a magnificent, loving God, you will begin to see that jumping from a ledge to «*end problems*'' will no longer appear feasible. Its facade will no longer have the power to overtake you. In Christ, there is no greater place of peace, regardless of the storm, stemming from the liberty found only in knowing and consigning your life to Yahweh. That proverbial ledge will be revealed for what it is—of Satan.

Whatever mess you›ve concocted, whatever trial besets you, no matter what is happening or for whatever reason, when you submit unto death the nature of the flesh, God commands Himself to take what Satan means against you for evil and turn it for good. I›ve quoted this Scripture a million times over, yet I will continue to do so because many folks still don›t get it. In Christ, there is no dilemma, only benefits from His Kingdom solution. Every horrible, disastrous, despicable situation is a platform God utilizes to catapult His people onto higher ground.

For more detailed information on this matter, I suggest reading the Bible beginning with the gospels to follow the life of Christ, the One who overcame death, grave, and every temptation known to man. He overcame the flesh while living in it. Once He is allowed to take over your life, you too will be able to do as He because His completed work will begin to manifest through you. Additionally, I have written numerous books elaborating on the subjects of knowing your identity in Christ, who you are in the Kingdom of God, how to draw closer to the heart of God, and much more.

If you learn nothing else from this, know that God is in love with you and always will be. He formed you in your mother's womb. He allowed your life to be spared thus far. There is life beyond this crisis. There is joy beyond this sorrow. There is acceptance beyond your rejections. There is gain after your loss. There is life outside death. Be encouraged and of good cheer, for Christ is in love with you today!

Author's Catalog

What was God Thinking?
Looking for God, 3 volumes or complete series
Discovering the Person of Holy Spirit, 4 volumes or complete series
How to Get it Right: Being Single, Married, Divorced and Everything in Between
Thy Kingdom Come: Kingdom vs. Religion
Holiness or Heresy: The Modern-Day Church
Navigating the Fiery Black Holes of Life: A Book of Faith
Talking Yourself off the Ledge: Encouragement at a Glance
Walking the Path of Freedom
When All My Strength has Failed
Wielding the Sword of the Spirit
Learning to Digest the Truth
Marriage Beyond Mediocrity
Wise as a Serpent, Innocent as a Dove
Philadelphia
Casting
Extinguishing the Inferno of Anger
Wrecked by My Ex
The War
Understanding Kingdom Prayer
Out of Obscurity
Gauchos, God, and Great Expectations
Holy Spirit Baptism for Baptists: And Anyone Else

The Fiery Sword Global Ministries
The Fiery Sword Publications
Lexington, SC 29073

www.thefierysword.com
thefierysword@windstream.net